BUS OPERATORS:1
Midland Red

MIDLAND
RED
HA-3667

BUS OPERATORS: 1
Midland Red

Malcolm Keeley

IAN ALLAN LTD

Title page: QC type char-a-banc. *Midland Red*

Contents

Cover: D7 No 4517 prepares to descend Gorcott Hill whilst on a Studley short working on the 148 service from Birmingham in July 1968. *MRK*

First published 1983

ISBN 0 7110 1316 0

Published by Ian Allan Ltd, Shepperton, Surrey; and printed by Ian Allan Printing Ltd at their works at Coombelands in Runnymede, England

Introduction

Many readers' interest in buses will have been sparked off by a new type of Midland Red vehicle, its gleaming flanks almost certainly hiding a technical specification bristling with revolutionary ideas. This initial introduction to the fascination of the company may then have received further encouragement by the acquisition of the latest edition of Ian Allan's *ABC Midland Red Buses and Coaches*. Sadly the publisher no longer produces this trusty volume but, in its day, your first 'ref' inevitably prompted in turn an investment in a 'Day Anywhere' ticket. With one of these, the young Midland Red afficionado could then venture into the obscurer reaches of the Company's vast territory and many will recall the excitement of peering into an unfamiliar garage and discovering some relic of the past lingering on in the ancillary fleet. These surprises were always a source of almost total mystery because even the Ian Allan 'ref' did not carry details of them (an omission rectified in the final editions). Neither did the Company's own fleet list with its discreet pink cover, which those 'in the know' possessed.

To those who grew up in the days before family car ownership became commonplace, the bright red service buses offered not only immense style but also the glamour of far away places. Midland Red was, after all, the largest bus company in England. To a Brummie, towns like Shrewsbury, Hereford and Banbury seemed a long, long way away. The coaches, naturally, travelled much further — the shiny red and black ambassadors of the company could be seen anywhere between John o'Groats and Lands End.

Things are different now, of course. The Sunday and Bank Holiday bus services to places of scenic interest are almost extinct. Before World War 2, their delights were splendidly promoted by special company travel guides and individual leaflets. These places subsequently became an easy ride in the household car but perhaps extinction is not inevitable — in these days of recession and rising petrol prices, the infant Midland Red (North) company is rigorously promoting the idea of family travel on its Sunday services to scenic spots. Coaching is different too in the motorway age. Long gone are the days when the London to Llandudno service would make a special stop near Rhuddlan for the passengers to inspect Bodelwyddan Church.

Every follower of Midland Red will have his or her cherished memories, the individuals or vehicles involved depending on one's age — like the first holiday away from parental guidance when an S14 was discovered at work on a bus service in distant Oswestry, highlighting the size of the company's operations; or making one's first trip down the motorway, relaxing aboard the local independent's Bedford coach and admiring its speed until a CM5T loped past so effortlessly that your steed seemed to be standing still; or savouring the technical strides of the D9 and the CM5T and then, on a special visit to Central Works, entering the experimental shop to be shown, without warning, the first D10! The writer eventually had the privilege to drive BMMO buses on a part-time basis and, even now, would exchange any present-day offering for a D9 — despite their apparent lack of brakes!

Three men dominate the Midland Red story and are referred to several times in this book. Messrs Shire and Power are entitled to the credit of building up the Company to its position of strength enjoyed upon the outbreak of World War 2. The writer recommends the reminiscences of Mr R. Tuft and Mr E. W. Suddrick in Midland Red's staff magazines of a quarter of a century ago which amply provide the flavour of the years between the two world wars when the company's buses released the less well-to-do from the confines of their native areas. The third man is Mr Donald Sinclair, the brilliant Scottish engineer who must have relished working with the fine

team, particularly the highly skilled design staff, left to him by Messrs Shire and Power. I am also happy to acknowledge the men and women at all levels who assisted these three 'giants' in the proudest years of the company and struggled on as times got harder for the bus industry.

This book follows the Midland Red story from the earliest days to beyond the division of the company in 1981. The development of the Midland Red bus is also described in as much detail as space allowed but exhaustive coverage was not possible.

The real Midland Red has now gone but, fortunately, its spirit lives on at the Midland Bus Museum, established at Wythall, nine miles south of Birmingham. Midland Red buses of all ages are being restored there by voluntary labour, alongside vehicles from other local operators, to show future generations of visitors their transport heritage. The significance of Midland Red in the engineering field will be clearly obvious because, happily, the Museum collection includes examples of such milestones as the Standard SOS, the S6 and the D10.

A few notes about fleet numbers are essential. Before World War 2 each vehicle had a bonnet number, generally coinciding with the last digits

Above: An early postwar scene at Evesham showing IM6 No HA 8297, a 1933 bus which gave 18 years' service. The post-1944 fleet number 1421, is unusually positioned on the bonnet side. *BaMMOT collection*

Above right: Midland Express, one name and livery to cover limited-stop stage services out of Birmingham irrespective of company, was launched on 28 March 1983. Midland Red (West) Leyland Leopard/Plaxton No 735, resplendent on the first day in its new livery of white with yellow band and red detail, overtakes one of five hired MAN articulated buses at Redditch Transport Interchange. *MRK*

of the registration. The company seemed loath to issue numbers far beyond 1,000 so the system worked well until the fleet size exceeded 1,000 vehicles when duplication of numbers began to occur. In 1923 the company had begun a private identification number series, backdated to 1915, for record purposes. These were known as the 'A' numbers and were adopted as fleet numbers from March 1944. Unfortunately, the 'A' numbers were rather jumbled amongst the older surviving stock and many people continued to refer to prewar vehicles by their registrations. Younger readers, however, will have always identified such vehicles, if they knew them at all, by their 'A' numbers. Thus the writer has referred to prewar vehicles by their 'A' numbers on the postwar photographs only, and the aggrieved will have to forgive the compromise. Postwar vehicles started very neatly at 3000, leaving numbers 2591 to 2999 vacant. This number series went up to 6473 when, in 1972, the company computer presumably ran out of fingers to count upon and reverted to 101. Secondhand vehicles purchased in recent years have used 2000 series numbers.

The writer wishes to thank all the photographers who have contributed to this volume — their work is acknowledged under each caption. Other gentlemen whose contributions are not so easily recognised include Peter Hardy and Stan Letts, who have checked the facts and, at the same time, valiantly tried to introduce correct English language where it was sadly lacking. Peter in particular knew the Midland Red story already, having been researching the Company's history for many years, and I am pleased to record the debt that I, and others who have delved into the past, owe to him. Any errors that have crept through, however, are almost certainly my responsibility. Further thanks go to Brian Baker, who kindly allowed access to his extensive collection of Midland Red photographs; to Mike Rooum, who bravely permitted me to borrow his irreplaceable collection of splendid prewar Midland Red literature, some of which is reproduced in this book; to Arthur Whitehouse for responding promptly and without complaint to my demands for the rapid printing of negatives; and to my regular partner-in-crime, Paul Gray, whose advice throughout and efforts on retouching certain grim but irresistible photographs was much valued.

Malcolm Keeley

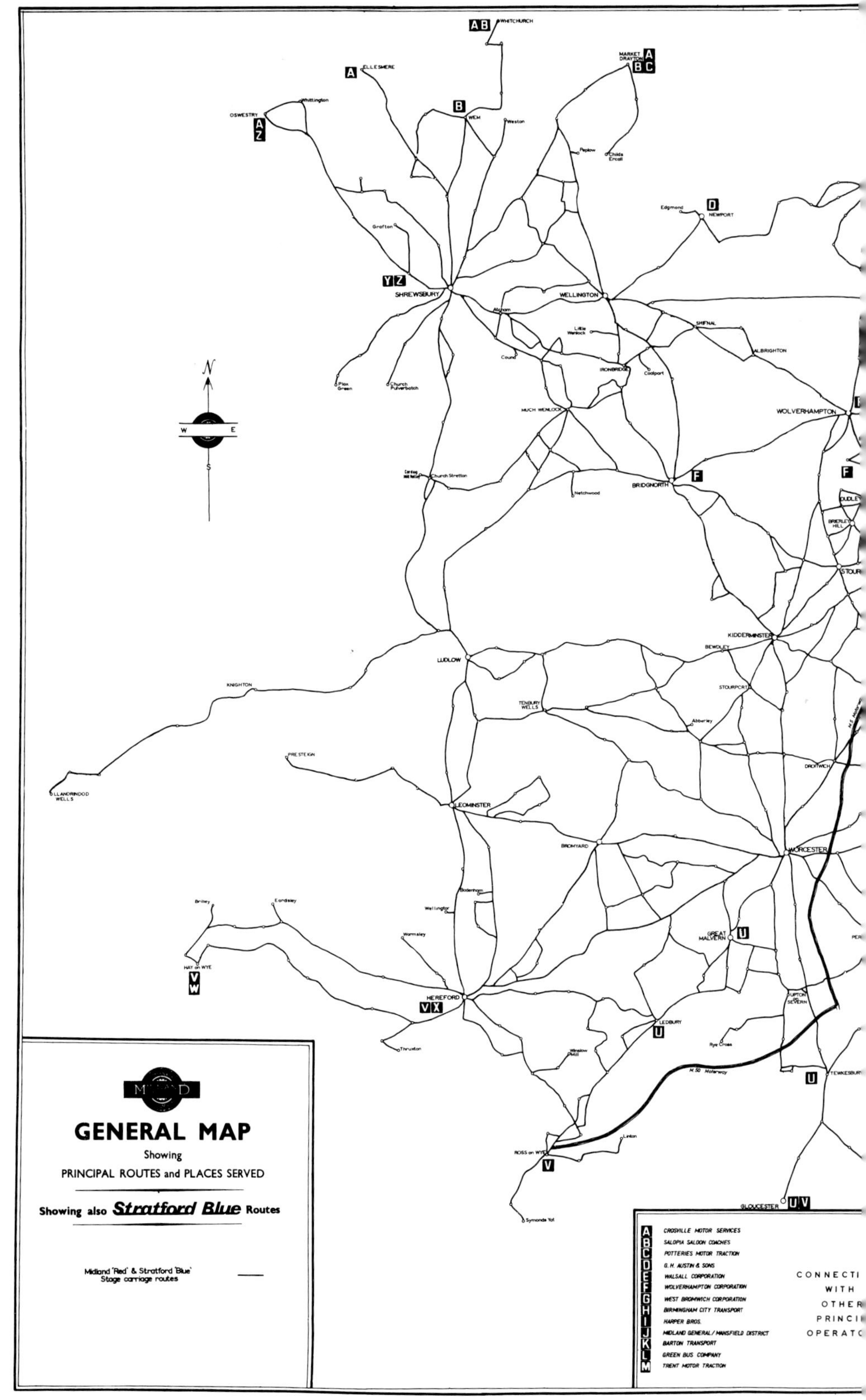
GENERAL MAP
Showing
PRINCIPAL ROUTES and PLACES SERVED
Showing also Stratford Blue Routes
Midland 'Red' & Stratford 'Blue' Stage carriage routes
SHREWSBURY
WELLINGTON
WOLVERHAMPTON
BRIDGNORTH
KIDDERMINSTER
LUDLOW
LEOMINSTER
BROMYARD
WORCESTER
HEREFORD
LEDBURY
ROSS on WYE
GLOUCESTER
TEWKESBURY
A CROSVILLE MOTOR SERVICES
B SALOPIA SALOON COACHES
C POTTERIES MOTOR TRACTION
D G.H. AUSTIN & SONS
E WALSALL CORPORATION
F WOLVERHAMPTON CORPORATION
G WEST BROMWICH CORPORATION
H BIRMINGHAM CITY TRANSPORT
I HARPER BROS.
J MIDLAND GENERAL / MANSFIELD DISTRICT
K BARTON TRANSPORT
L GREEN BUS COMPANY
M TRENT MOTOR TRACTION

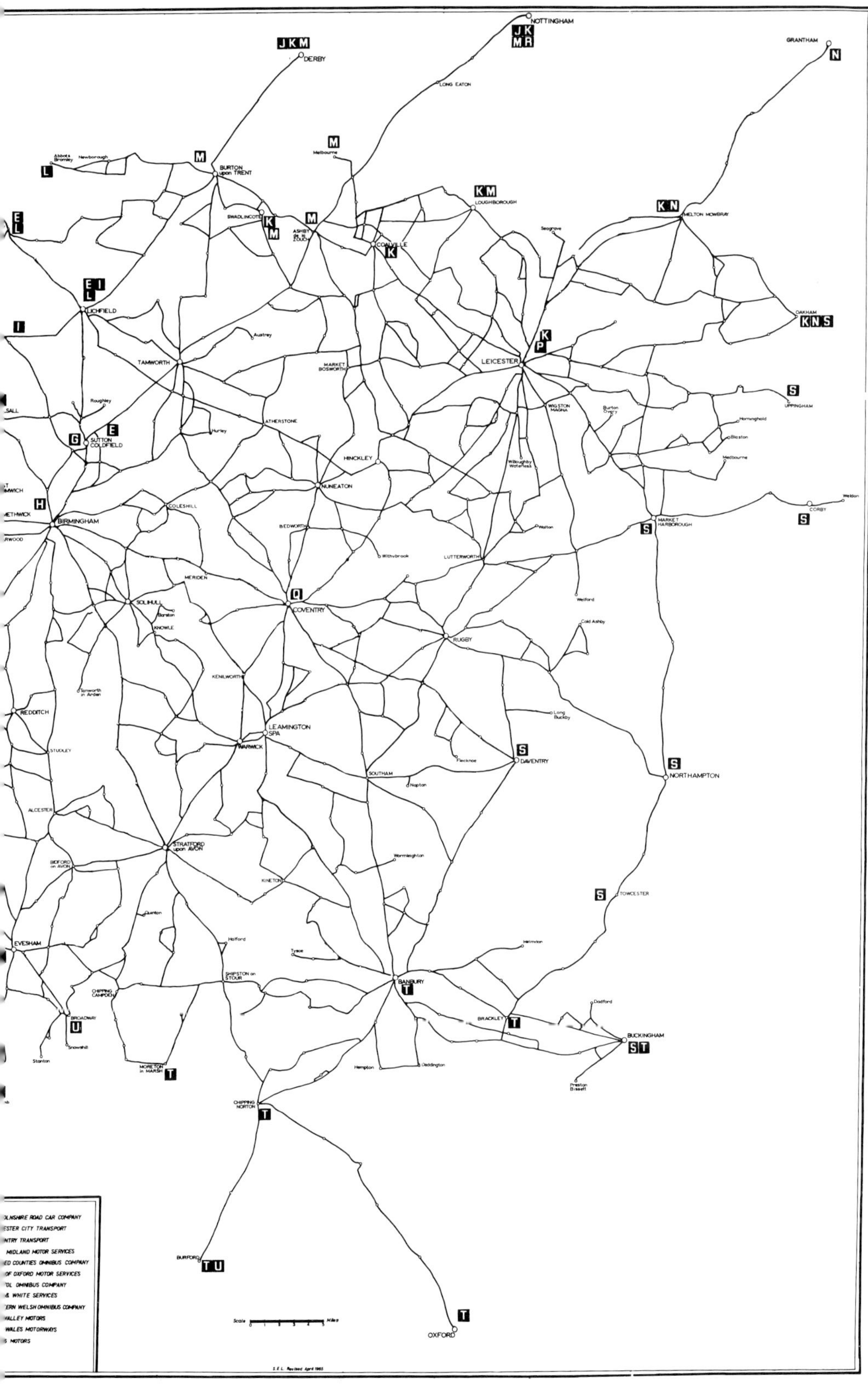

From Motor Buses to Horse Buses

By 1903 the British Electric Traction Company Ltd, then with extensive transport interests throughout the country, held a monopoly of the tramway and horse omnibus companies in the Birmingham area. That year the privately owned Birmingham Motor Express Company Ltd entered the scene as an operator of motor omnibuses. The enterprise lacked capital so, on 26 November 1904, a new company was registered whose shares were to be available to the general public. This was the Birmingham & Midland Motor Omnibus Company Ltd, the proper name of the 'Midland Red' until 1974.

The fledgling company did not attract the anticipated interest and in June 1905 all but one of the directors resigned, to be replaced by nominees of the BET, which was prepared to provide the necessary finance. Thus Midland Red became part of the BET empire. At this time BMMO officially took over the 15 motor omnibuses of Birmingham Motor Express and also

Below: One of the new 1904 Milnes-Daimlers of Birmingham Motor Express attracts attention in New Street, Birmingham. The inquisitive gentleman at the front would not be the last to peer at the mechanics of these early machines.

Left: One of the more powerful 24hp Milnes-Daimlers, seen following acquisition by BMMO, and after repainting at the Kyotts Lake Road, Birmingham, depot of the Birmingham & Midland Joint Tramways Committee. This view clearly shows the conversion to chain-drive which replaced the original rack-and-pinion mechanism.

Below: The first new buses purchased by BMMO under BET control were nine of these Brush 'B' types, delivered between October 1906 and January 1907. This view is also taken at Kyotts Lake Road depot.

the horse omnibuses and four motor buses (introduced to compete with the BME) of the BET tramway subsidiaries in Birmingham.

Some of the motor buses were replaced by newer vehicles in 1906 but their maintenance proved a continual problem. Therefore in October 1907 all the motor buses were withdrawn from service in Birmingham. They were transferred, mostly to Deal in Kent, but a few to Warwick, still remaining the property of BMMO until sold in 1910 to the British Automobile Development Company Ltd, the BET's subsidiary specifically for motor bus activities. The Birmingham and Midland MOTOR Omnibus Company thus came to operate only horse omnibuses, a reversal of most company histories!

Motor Buses Return to Stay

The influence of the BET subsidiaries in Birmingham had waned considerably by 1912, as the tramway leases had expired and the services within the city were now being operated by new corporation electric tramcars, only routes from points outside the boundary being left to the BET companies. It had always been a condition of the licences issued by the Birmingham Watch Committee that omnibuses should not run over tramway routes and, thus, as the corporation tramways were extended, so the corresponding horse bus services were withdrawn. By 1911, the BMMO company's activities were virtually restricted to the Harborne and Hagley Road routes and it was here that, in May 1912, motor buses were tried again. These were petrol-electric vehicles of Tilling-Stevens manufacture, which proved easy for former horse bus drivers to handle, as they had no gearboxes, and were much more successful than their predecessors. All horse bus operations were soon superseded and the following year motor bus services were opened up in districts just outside Birmingham.

On 5 September 1913 Birmingham Corporation opened an electric tramway along the Hagley Road, which was thus placed 'out of bounds' to BMMO buses, and it was obvious that something would have to be done to avoid further conflict between the two parties. Negotiations led to a highly successful agreement between BMMO and Birmingham Corporation in February 1914, whereby the company would not compete with the corporation within the city boundary and the corporation would not compete with the company outside. This involved the takeover in October by the corporation of the company's operations wholly in the city, including a garage and 30 double-deck motor buses, while the company removed its headquarters to Bearwood and began to build up a network of services from central Birmingham to points outside the city boundary, giving protection to the corporation services.

Operations based on other towns began upon the outbreak of World War 1. Many vehicles of other companies were requisitioned by the War Office but, because the Tilling-Stevens petrol-electric system was not approved of initially, BMMO kept its fleet intact. Thus BMMO was able to step in when both associated and rival companies had to withdraw facilities.

Right: Motor bus operation resumed in May 1912 with Tilling-Stevens TTA1 vehicles like O 8208. The upper-deck passenger towards the rear is Mr L. G. Wyndham Shire, newly appointed as Chief Engineer, who himself drove the first example on delivery from London to Birmingham.

Left: The more powerful Tilling-Stevens TTA2 was adopted in 1913, in both double- and single-deck form. O 9938 had a Birch rear-entrance body but BMMO then went on to standardise on front entrances because Mr Shire found such vehicles did not have to stop completely for loading or unloading!

Below left: The Tilling-Stevens TS3 was favoured by BMMO for a number of years. This 1914 example with 29-seat body is typical of its era, but hopefully its unscheduled excursion through a hedge and down an embankment was not.

Below: These Worcestershire Motor Transport 40hp Leylands were delivered in 1914 in red livery for use in Kidderminster (WMT buses in Worcester were green). The order to the signwriter must have been given by someone with a lisp because FK 539 appeared wrongly registered as SK 539. When the War Department requisitioned these chassis, Midland Red assumed operations, and used the Brush bodies on new Tilling-Stevens TS3 chassis obtained the following year.

Shire Power

Upon the return of peace, the company possessed a scattered network of routes and embarked upon a two-pronged policy of consolidating existing areas of operation and expanding into new ones. This necessitated the introduction of further operating agreements with municipal operators. It was an era of fearless investment and dynamic promotion of the company's services. It was the practice for a few buses, with the necessary staff to man them, to be despatched to a selected district and a network of routes built up with the minimum of facilities. Competition would be challenged, and, where practicable, eliminated. The author's favourite story comes from Leicester and tells of a 22-stone BMMO inspector who, spying an 'opposition' driver near a wall, 'accidentally' leant upon the unfortunate with his arm across the poor chap's windpipe until the next 'Red' bus was loaded and away! It is doubtful if it was intended that the opposition should be crushed so literally. The same heavyweight is reported to have rocked violently a small 'opposition' bus full of passengers from side to side because the driver had annoyed him!

Some mention of the gentlemen in charge of the company is appropriate at this point. Traffic matters had been under the wing of Mr O. C. Power from the outset and, from 1912, engineering had been the responsibility of Mr L. G. Wyndham Shire. There was no General Manager, yet the company prospered under this unusual management structure and the chemistry of two men who, apparently, very rarely saw eye to eye. An interesting by-product of this separation of interests was that drivers were under the aegis of Mr Shire and conductors under Mr Power, each with quite different uniforms of brown and blue respectively.

Some of the company's competitors were armed with small, fast, lightweight buses that ran proverbial rings around the 'Red' Tillings. Mr Shire was conscious of this shortcoming. Initial steps to meet the threat were the purchases of some small Fords and Garfords in 1921-2 which gave the company useful experience with lightweight vehicles. Mr Shire, however, required a straightforward design which combined the capacity of a full size single-decker with the nimbleness of a lightweight but the manufacturers could not provide such a machine.

The company was already obtaining mechanical items from the numerous engineering workshops in Birmingham and the Black Country and it was thus well placed when Mr Shire decided that BMMO should produce its own buses to meet its needs. The first model entered production in 1923 and was a normal control single-decker with high revving four-cylinder petrol engine, a reliable gearbox with plate clutch transmission, pneumatic tyres, and a body of lightweight timber construction. The company's products were known by the letters SOS, the initials are now widely believed to mean 'Shire's Omnibus Specification' — the vagueness surrounding the initials and the type letters which followed is typical of Wyndham Shire. The first model was known as the 'Standard SOS' and a considerable number were built. A minority were turned out as char-a-bancs, as had been a small number of earlier vehicles.

The company moved on to forward control buses in 1926 and a succession of types was produced over the next few years, offering steady improvements to the passenger in terms of capacity, entrance height and seating comfort. In 1929 Midland Red introduced its first fully enclosed coaches, a development which revolutionised this aspect of the company's operations. Six-cylinder engines became normal for long distance vehicles and an increasing number of similarly equipped machines were built alongside the traditional four-cylinder models for the service bus fleet.

Considerable numbers of SOS chassis were

supplied to certain associated BET companies in the period 1924-34, with bodies to Midland Red pattern. Trent Motor Traction continued to receive SOS chassis until 1940 although the later deliveries were fitted with bodies to Trent's own specification. Sales to other companies unfortunately were not resumed after World War 2.

The BET tramways in the Black Country had come under pressure from independent operators and, from 1926, they were gradually replaced by Midland Red buses. Worcester Corporation exercised its right to purchase the BET owned tramways within the city but, instead of operating tramcars, trolleybuses or replacement buses itself, the corporation entered into an agreement with Midland Red whereby new SOS buses took over from the tramcars on 1 June 1928.

This period saw large scale investment in bus companies by the railways and half the ordinary shares in BMMO were purchased in April 1930 by the Great Western Railway and the London, Midland & Scottish Railway. These shares passed to the state upon railway nationalisation in 1948. The Great Western Railway, a pioneer bus operator in its own right, possessed a few services in the area and these were taken over by Midland Red along with some buses, which were soon sold.

Also in April 1930, BMMO purchased Black & White Motorways Ltd of Cheltenham, a company specialising in long distance coach services. This undertaking remained separate, however, and its control was shared with two other companies. In 1934, BMMO became a major partner in 'Associated Motorways', the first step towards a nationwide, co-ordinated, network in which the Black & White coach station at Cheltenham became a focal point where coaches connected and passengers interchanged.

The Road Traffic Act, 1930, brought regulation to the industry and operators who obtained licences for services enjoyed the protection of the Traffic Commissioners. Gone were the days when independents could poach on the company's best routes, and similarly the 'Red' could no longer use its superior might to crush the opposition. Nevertheless the company continued to expand up until the outbreak of war in 1939 by the purchase of over 150 small businesses and their services.

Important purchases in 1935 included two companies of the Midland Counties Electric Supply Company, ie the Leamington & Warwick Transport Company and Stratford-upon-Avon Blue Motors Ltd. Midland Red buses took over at Leamington and Warwick in 1937 but Stratford Blue was retained as a subsidiary for many years. Surprisingly, Midland Red-built buses were not normally supplied to the Stratford company which standardised initially on secondhand Tilling-Stevens and, from 1948, on new Leylands. Another significant acquisition was the Leicester & District Bus Company in 1936, some of whose green Albions were operated for a short time, an unusual occurrence with Midland Red.

The company had operated some Tilling-Stevens double-deckers between 1922 and 1929 but, since then, had depended entirely on single-deck buses. Traffic requirements necessitated a rethink, however, and a rear-entrance double-

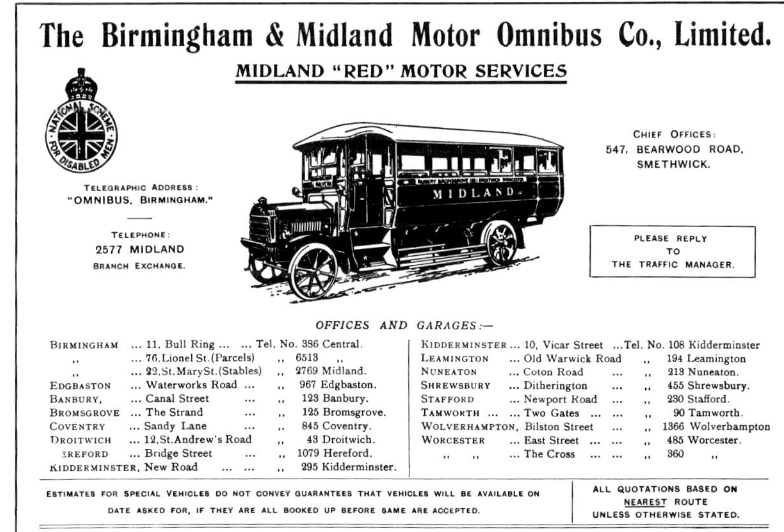
The Birmingham & Midland Motor Omnibus Co., Limited.

MIDLAND "RED" MOTOR SERVICES

TELEGRAPHIC ADDRESS: "OMNIBUS, BIRMINGHAM."

TELEPHONE: 2577 MIDLAND BRANCH EXCHANGE.

CHIEF OFFICES: 547, BEARWOOD ROAD, SMETHWICK.

PLEASE REPLY TO THE TRAFFIC MANAGER.

OFFICES AND GARAGES:—

BIRMINGHAM	... 11, Bull Ring ...	... Tel. No. 386 Central.
,,	... 76, Lionel St. (Parcels)	,, 6513 ,,
,,	... 22, St. Mary St. (Stables)	,, 2769 Midland.
EDGBASTON	... Waterworks Road ...	,, 967 Edgbaston.
BANBURY,	... Canal Street ...	,, 123 Banbury.
BROMSGROVE	... The Strand ...	,, 125 Bromsgrove.
COVENTRY	... Sandy Lane ...	,, 845 Coventry.
DROITWICH	... 12, St. Andrew's Road	,, 43 Droitwich.
[H]EREFORD	... Bridge Street ...	,, 1079 Hereford.
KIDDERMINSTER,	New Road	,, 295 Kidderminster.
KIDDERMINSTER	... 10, Vicar Street	...Tel. No. 108 Kidderminster
LEAMINGTON	... Old Warwick Road	,, 194 Leamington
NUNEATON	... Coton Road ...	,, 213 Nuneaton.
SHREWSBURY	... Ditherington ...	,, 455 Shrewsbury.
STAFFORD	... Newport Road ...	,, 230 Stafford.
TAMWORTH ...	... Two Gates	,, 90 Tamworth.
WOLVERHAMPTON,	Bilston Street ...	,, 1366 Wolverhampton
WORCESTER	... East Street	,, 485 Worcester.
,, ,,	... The Cross	,, 360 ,,

ESTIMATES FOR SPECIAL VEHICLES DO NOT CONVEY GUARANTEES THAT VEHICLES WILL BE AVAILABLE ON DATE ASKED FOR, IF THEY ARE ALL BOOKED UP BEFORE SAME ARE ACCEPTED.

ALL QUOTATIONS BASED ON NEAREST ROUTE UNLESS OTHERWISE STATED.

Your reference C.O.S/P.B.

Right: The company letterhead as used in 1922. Both the wording and the bus would be updated regularly.

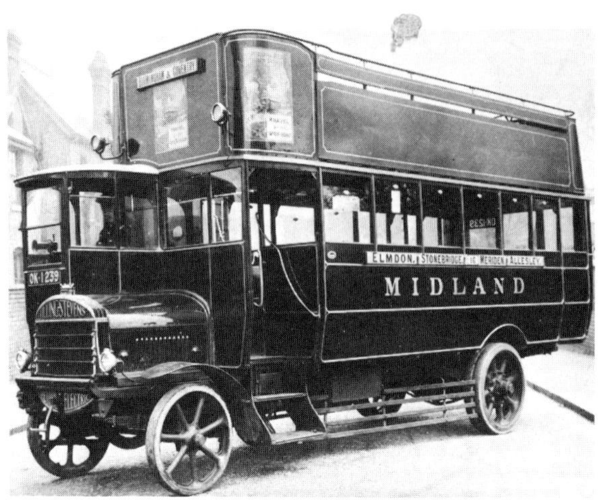

Below: **The interior of a 1919 TS3, OE 1137. Distinctly spartan although the high gloss of the woodwork is impressive. Note the partition towards the rear, behind which smoking was permitted. The bodies were built to BMMO specification, in this case by Brush.**

Below right: **A chilly scene at Chipping Norton showing 1920 Tilling-Stevens TS3 OE 6176. The body design is of a revised style, without over-light windows, and taking the shape later to become familiar on SOS vehicles. Delivered with solid tyres and electric transmission, this machine is seen after conversion to pneumatics and SOS four-speed 'crash' gearbox. Many later Tillings were similarly modified. The bus declares an intention to run to Deddington and Banbury. It was withdrawn in 1931.**

Above: **A fleet of Tilling-Stevens double-deckers was constructed between 1922 and 1924, using TS3 chassis converted to forward control. The 51-seat bodies were built at Carlyle Road Works — the choice of front entrance was typically BMMO but unusual for the period. The company decided to standardise on single-deckers only in 1928, when the great majority of these vehicles were withdrawn. Eighteen bodies were rebuilt in 1929 as single-decker buses and fitted to SOS FS chassis whose char-a-banc bodies were already out of date.** *Midland Red*

deck prototype appeared in 1931. A production batch of 50 similar double-deckers appeared in 1932-3. Midland Red then began, somewhat unusually, to standardise on front-entrance double-deckers, well over 300 such vehicles being added to the fleet by 1939.

The double-deckers had six-cylinder engines which also became standard for all single-deckers from 1934. Early 1930s buses were still petrol powered, however, and naturally Mr Shire was becoming interested in the economical diesel engined vehicles then appearing throughout the country. After a few experimental vehicles, batches of SOS single-deckers with AEC diesel engines were built in 1935-6 for the Midland Red and Trent fleets. The company was able to put its own diesel engine into production in 1936, a compact design of eight litres capacity, and a number of petrol vehicles was subsequently converted to diesel with these units.

The front engine position continued to be favoured throughout this period but the batches of coaches built in 1937 and 1939 had full width cabs to streamline their appearance. Three double-deckers were similarly equipped although the effect failed to make the same impression! Important exceptions to the rule were four rear-engined prototypes built in 1935-6, comprising three single-deck buses and one coach. The quartet were not particularly successful, which is not surprising bearing in mind their highly experimental nature, but one has to admire Mr Shire and the Company for their boldness in this field.

The outbreak of war in September 1939 brought an end to the production of SOS buses. The next chapter will show that, by the time peace returned, the management of the company was in new hands and the vehicles produced rather different. In the meantime, BMMO and its employees went to war.

MIDLAND "RED"
MOTOR SERVICES.

ROUTE GUIDE SERVICE No. 133

Birmingham to Coventry

2665

HAS anyone ever threatened to "send you to Coventry?"

If so, you realise that, for some reason or other, you have merited their displeasure, and that you are to be punished therefor.

Next time anyone uses the threat to me I shall certainly reply that, if the journey is to be made by a "Midland Red," I shall be prepared to take my punishment like a man.

Above: Four-sided route guides were produced for a number of services, this being the front page of the one for the Birmingham to Coventry route, then numbered 133. The use of the swastika as a patterned surround was not unusual until its adoption by the German Nazis.

Above right: One of the two Model T Fords acquired in 1921. The char-a-banc bodies would seat 11.

Right: The Garfords were received in bus and char-a-banc form and entered service in 1922. They had short lives, being withdrawn in 1925, but gave the company valuable experience in the construction of fast, lightweight, vehicles. *Midland Red*

Below right: One of the first batch of 'Standard SOS' buses, built in 1923. The 32-seat body was built by Brush to BMMO specification. The 1923-4 production used Tilling chassis frames. *Midland Red*

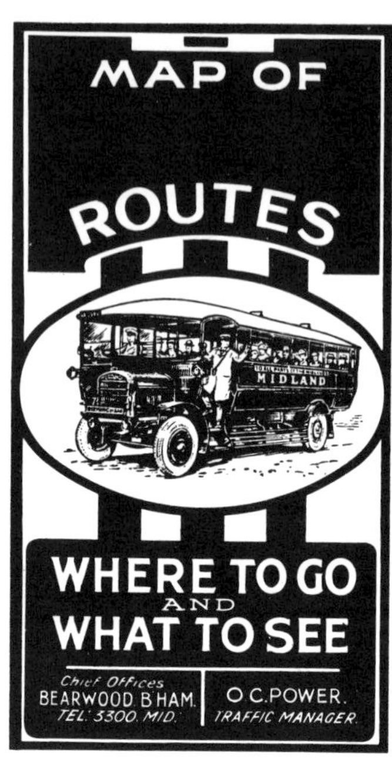

Above: The FS model was produced in 1926, the type letters are believed to mean Forward Steering, or possibly Future Standard. This photograph of HA 3546 is a delightful period piece, with the White Hart Hotel to the rear offering good stabling. The destination board reads 'Coventry via Atherstone & Nuneaton'.

Above right: Mid-20s route map with prototype FS No HA 2500 on the cover.

Below: Like preceding types of vehicle, some 'Standards' were turned out with char-a-banc bodies. For several years Davidson of Trafford Park received the contracts to build the company's char-a-banc requirements. *Midland Red*

Above: The 1927 production consisted of the Q (Queen) model. The front bulkhead was moved forward as far as possible, enabling 37 seats to be fitted, compared to 34 of the FS. This reduced the length of the driver's cab somewhat although some compensation was achieved by moving the engine, bonnet and radiator slightly towards the nearside. This assymetric arrangement would remain a feature of all subsequent SOS half-cab designs. HA 3600 is seen at Grantham in August 1933 — by which time the driver was able to enjoy the benefit of front as well as the original rear wheel braking. *G. H. F. Atkins*

Above right: Colour cover, dating from around 1930 and featuring a QL, of a 176-page guide to, seemingly, every nook and cranny in the Midlands.

Below: The adoption of twin rear wheels, smaller in size than hitherto, enabled a significantly lower frame height on the QL (Queen Low), introduced in 1928. Four-wheel brakes became standard. HA 3726 is seen here in Swadlincote. Such was the intense pride of the period that conductors were issued with dusters with which to wipe from the leather seats the dust from contemporary roads, while drivers were issued with black tyre-wall paint to keep up appearances in that department. Withdrawal of QLs began in 1937 (a nine-year life was normal in prewar years) but some were still around upon the outbreak of war and were to be seen in service in diminishing numbers until 1950!
C. D. Wilkinson collection

Right: Coach design continued to evolve. After experience with FS chars-a-banc, the Company reverted to normal control for the QC model (Queen Charabanc). The QC was primarily intended for touring work and, of course, the normal control layout meant the return of the driver to the passenger compartment. Gone were the individual doors to each row of seats, the single door at the front enabling fixed side windows to be fitted which, together with the fixed rear dome, eased the erection of the hood in inclement weather.

The QLC was evolved from the QC — the vehicle shown, HA 4835, being one of the 1928 delivery. Subsequent batches were built in 1929 and 1930 but had six-cylinder engines and an improved radiator design. *Midland Red*

Below right: The M class at last brought significant improvements for the bus passenger. The type letter stood for Madam (the buses were designed to attract lady shoppers etc), and more comfortable seating was fitted. Despite the removal of the central partition, the capacity of the bus was reduced to 34. Note the gently curved sides and sloping windscreen, the latter feature standard on later QLs. The mechanical specification was similar to the QL. *Midland Red*

Bottom right: The first totally enclosed long distance coach was the XL (Excel) class of 1929-30 powered by six-cylinder engines. Unfortunately the lightweight chassis could not cope with the weight, and the engines were too small, so the decision was taken to re-chassis the vehicles. The result was the highly successful RR (Rolls-Royce) class, a beefier design with a more powerful engine. The coaches seated 30. *Midland Red*

Above right: The MM (Modified Madam) four-cylinder type had succeeded the M later in 1929. However, after about a dozen had entered service, the bodies were lifted and refitted to the six-cylinder chassis originally fitted to the XL coaches. The rest of the former XL chassis, plus 10 new chassis, were similarly bodied. The MM type thus became a six-cylinder model in the Midland Red fleet. *Roy Marshall*

Below: One of the early 'standard' SOS buses was rebodied in 1929 as a prototype for improved stock on the less busy routes. The resulting vehicle was reclassified ODD (the meaning is uncertain), and was followed by a production batch of 50 rebuilds. The original bodies, which were not life expired, were transferred to some of the surviving Tilling-Stevens buses. HA 2450 is seen here in Worcester Street, Birmingham outside the Midland Red enquiry office. This area has been demolished and is now partly occupied by the Rotunda. The ODD class, which seated 26, was generally withdrawn from passenger service in 1938. *John E. Brown*

Above: SOS developments were certainly confused about this time. A further class, the COD (Clarke's Own Design — Clarke was Chief Engineer of Trent Motor Traction) appeared in 1930. This type had longer windows, reducing the number of bays by one, and the interior finish reflected the desire to use the vehicles on longer bus services. However the production examples had four-cylinder engines and Midland Red must have found them somewhat short-winded because another body swapping programme was instituted! Two new classes were formed — the IM (later IM4, Improved Madam four-cylinder), featuring the four-cylinder chassis from the original MM and the COD classes fitted with new bodies — and the IM6 (IM six-cylinder), featuring new six-cylinder chassis with bodies from the COD class. Subsequently a large number of totally new IM4 and IM6 vehicles was added. HA 6192 was one of a Short-bodied batch built in 1931 and is seen in Nottingham two years later. The IM class was generally withdrawn between 1948 and 1952. The COD type survived in the Trent and Potteries fleets and was thus associated with them. *G. H. F. Atkins*

Below left: Folding maps were produced in the 1930s for services of exceptional scenic interest.

Below : The return of double-deckers to the fleet was heralded by this prototype machine, HA 7329, which entered service in 1931. The Short-bodied vehicle is seen at Stourbridge. Note the curious appearance caused by the lack of an orthodox destination display. *R. T. Wilson*

Left: Fifty more double-deckers followed in 1932-3. They were originally classified DD (Double-Decker) but, after reclassification to DD(RE) in 1934, they eventually became best known as REDD (Rear Entrance Double Decker). The body contract was shared between four builders, HA 8004 being a Short-bodied example. It is seen at Rose Bank Gardens, Great Malvern. *R. T. Wilson*

Below left: The ON (Onward) class, which first appeared later in 1934, took advantage of the then maximum permitted length of 27ft 6in. This, combined with the compact engine and cab layout enabled 38 passengers to be seated comfortably in a single-decker. The RR2SB (IM6 type) engine was fitted. AHA 489, with Short body, is seen at Woodgate — note the improved front end styling. *G. B. Sampson*

Below: Three designs of six-cylinder engine were already in use, the SS (fitted to some OLC coaches and the MM class), the RR2SB (the IM6 class) and the RR2LB (the RR family and DD class). Now another type was evolved for the BRR (Bus Rolls-Royce), of which the production batch of 20 entered service in 1934. Their more rounded body style had also appeared on late examples of the IM family. Short-bodied HA 9387 is seen at Leicester bearing fleet No 1490, issued under the 1944 numbering scheme. *R. A. Mills*

Right: Following experiments with various makes of diesel engine, a number of SOS chassis were produced in 1935-6 with AEC 7.7litre engines, classified DON (Diesel ON). This example was supplied to Trent and is very similar to those of Midland Red except for the roller destination blind — a luxury which BMMO found hard to adopt! The length of the AEC engine meant a longer bonnet and cab, the compensating reduction to 36 seats in the passenger compartment being given away by the shorter bay behind the entrance. *W. J. Haynes*

Below right: A new double-deck design was evolved in 1933 and was originally classified DD(FE) — Double Decker (Front Entrance). They soon became better known as the FEDD type, arguably the most famous Midland Red model of all. The first 50 production vehicles entered service in 1934 with Short bodies of traditional composite construction. HA 9402 shows the original livery and lining of these vehicles. The Short-bodied FEDDs were generally withdrawn between 1948 and 1950, apart from a handful with rebuilt bodies which lasted until 1953. *R. T. Wilson*

Below: 135 further FEDDs joined the Midland Red fleet in 1935-6. Although very similar in appearance, these BHA registered vehicles had all-metal Metro-Cammell bodies. These proved very durable, surviving in service without major rebuilding until withdrawal between 1953 and 1957. All these early FEDDs had RR2LB petrol engines, apart from a couple of diesel experiments. The Metro-Cammell vehicles were converted to diesel, however, between 1942 and 1947 with either AEC 7.7litre or BMMO engines. *BaMMOT collection*

Go by Road for your Works & Staff Outings

SEND P.C. FOR

PRIVATE PARTY TOUR BOOK

FINE SELECTION OF ITINERARIES TO THE SEA AND POPULAR INLAND PLEASURE RESORTS.

Call at the nearest Office or Agency for Quotation

Arrangements can be made, if desired, for Representatives to Attend Outings Committees.

CHEAPER RATES FOR MID-WEEK DAY BOOKINGS

Travel by Coach

Below: A new style of coach was evolved for production in 1934-5. This was the LRR (Low Rolls-Royce) which incorporated a low, double-deck type, chassis. The low height emphasised the length of the coaches and was a design fad of the time, as was the garish livery. AHA 608 prepares to leave the Cheltenham coach station of Black & White en route to Wolverhampton, whilst the Red & White behind will travel to Birmingham only. This highly evocative scene shows the old Associated Motorways network in action — not a white National coach to be seen. *C. F. Martin collection*

Above: New touring coaches were also produced in 1935, to replace some of the ageing OLCs. The normal control layout continued to be favoured for such duties and the result was the 29-seat OLR (Open Low Rolls-Royce), of which 25 were built. One suspects that, with their long bonnets and canvas roofs, they were out-of-date even as they were built. AHA 630 is seen down south in the company of London Transport AEC Renown LT 811. Short built the bodies on both the LRR and OLR classes. *J. F. Higham*

Right: Years away from the OLR in design were the four rear-engined prototypes produced in 1935-6. The first is seen here. The official designation was REC (Rear Engined Coach) although only one, CHA 1, was actually a coach. Six-cylinder petrol engines were fitted and the bodies were built by Carlyle. The main problem with these vehicles was that the swirl of air at the rear caused dirt to get into the engine, despite care with filtration, resulting in excessive cylinder wear. *Midland Red*

Below right: The first production vehicles with the Company's own 'K' ('Kidney') 8litre diesel engine were 65 SON (Saloon Onward) class, built in 1936-7 with 39-seat bodies by English Electric. They included two new features, a sliding entrance door, and an off-side emergency exit which facilitated the fitting of the extra seat along the back row. These buses were thus instantly recognisable from the rear by the two large back windows instead of the usual three. Many of the earlier ON type were fitted with 'K' diesel engines in 1937-8 and were re-classified CON (Converted ON).

Below: Fifty more coaches, with bodies by English Electric, were built for the 1937 season and were designated SLR (Saloon Low Rolls-Royce). These were splendid looking machines with full-width cabs and oozing 1930s charm. The smooth lines were marred only by the stepped waistrail, a typical feature of the period. The livery was red with maroon trim. A remarkable lapse of attention to detail, but reflecting the company's attitude to such things perhaps, was the angle of the destination screens — surely unreadable to anyone less than nine feet tall! This defect was soon rectified, however. Like many other operators, smooth petrol engines continued to be favoured for the coach fleet — RR2LB units being fitted in this case.

Above: The next batch of SONs, built 1937-8, 100 in all and carrying DHA registrations, reverted to the standard 'porch' entrance arrangement and rear emergency door. However a number of SLR influences were evident, eg the tapered window pillars and maroon flash (ill suited to the straight bus lines), and the fuel tank in a sensible place instead of under the driver's seat! The bodies were again built by English Electric. This unidentified example must have been almost new when seen at the Bull Ring terminus, Birmingham, outside St Martins Church. More batches of SONs were built in 1938-40, but lacked the ornate SLR influences. *R. T. Wilson*

Left: 150 further FEDDs were built in 1938-9, with composite bodies by Brush. SLR influence persisted on the first batch of 50 with the positioning of the fuel tanks and, in the case of three buses, the provision of full width cabs. The latter emphasised the offset radiators which on some vehicles, including EHA 290, were of a new style. The original livery is shown to good effect here. The three full cab buses were rebuilt to half cab in 1940

Right: A more typical EHA FEDD is seen here at Grantham in June 1950, in largely original condition apart from the livery. Note that the sliding door of the earlier FEDDs has been superseded by a jack-knife door in a recessed entrance. *G. H. F. Atkins*

Below right: The last new SOS type was the ONC (Onward Coach), of which 25 were constructed in 1939. 'K' 8litre engines were employed, these being the first diesel powered Company coaches. The bodies were built by Duple and survived virtually unchanged, apart from livery, until withdrawal around 1959-60. FHA 408 is seen at Digbeth during the 1950s. *S. E. Letts*

Below: The new style radiator design was adopted as standard, and the final batches of SONs and FEDDs had more rounded rear roof domes. This early postwar view of FHA 870, carrying fleet No 2366, also shows some evidence of lower deck rebuilding — a major programme would be undertaken later. The scene is High Street, Birmingham. *R. A. Mills*

Expansion and Contraction

Donald M. Sinclair joined Midland Red in 1940, initially as Chief Engineer succeeding Mr Wyndham Shire upon his retirement. The unfortunate death 'in harness' of Mr Power in 1943 brought an end to the unusual joint management structure with Mr Sinclair being appointed the company's first General Manager. Prior to joining Midland Red, Mr Sinclair had been Chief Engineer of Northern General Transport, the well known BET subsidiary in north-east England. NGT possessed a considerable fleet of SOS vehicles so the marque and its capabilities were not unknown to Mr Sinclair. Latterly, however, NGT had produced its own side-engined high-capacity single-deckers. He was hardly a stranger to innovation therefore and, to Mr Wyndham Shire's splendid but usually conservative work-horses, Mr Sinclair was to add style.

There was little opportunity for innovation upon his arrival, however. World War 2 had caused the suspension of vehicle manufacture, both inside and outside the company. The Ministry of Supply eventually permitted the limited production of buses by outside manufacturers and a small number of Leyland and AEC, followed by a larger quantity of Guy and Daimler, double-deckers entered what had been previously an all SOS fleet.

Mr Sinclair prepared for a return to normal manufacture. The four unsuccessful prewar rear engined vehicles were very extensively rebuilt into underfloor-engined single-deckers, to be joined by a fifth, entirely new, prototype. A new type code system was evolved and the five prototypes were styled S1 to S5. Mr Sinclair did not anticipate, at this stage, moving the engine on double-deckers from the traditional front position. However he modernised the appearance dramatically by restyling the front end, concealing the radiator, and using a grille which retained the family connection with the single-deck fleet. The first experiment in this direction used a prewar FEDD model but an entirely new prototype double-decker entered service in 1945, type coded D1. The new bus reverted to a rear entrance and the sleek body lines featured only four window bays on the lower deck, as adopted on the London RT.

Vehicle production resumed in 1946 and, over the next five years, 500 underfloor-engined single-deckers were produced that were clearly based on the wartime prototypes. The manufacturing name now became BMMO, the Company's initials, rather than SOS. Indeed the SOS insignia was removed from prewar vehicles although they continued to be called 'Sosses' by those who knew them.

It was unfortunate that Midland Red did not have the capacity to produce vehicles for other operators. The major manufacturers were not able to introduce underfloor-engined models for several years and BMMO was quite clearly ahead. Midland Red was unable, in fact, to meet its own needs and purchased 100 AEC Regent II chassis to receive double-deck bodies based on the D1 prototype. Arrival of these Regents from the bodybuilders was rather slow, however, indeed before delivery was completed, BMMO had a number of its own postwar double-deckers on the road. The second 100 of these featured another new innovation, electrically operated platform doors. Early postwar BMMO production also included 57 underfloor-engined coaches which were, again, years ahead in design and style.

Fleet renewal only proceeded slowly, despite all these new buses. Replacement of stock had virtually ceased during the war years so elderly vehicles ran well beyond their intended lives. The return of peace brought an unprecedented travel boom which particularly benefited public transport as private cars remained difficult to obtain and fuel was restricted. Midland Red thus had to retain in service every vehicle it could and the growth in the bus fleet had to be accompanied by

Above: Letterhead in use upon the outbreak of World War 2.

a programme of new garages and extensions. It was obvious that many prewar vehicles would be around for several more years and thus a large number of middle and late 1930s buses had their bodies extensively rehabilitated.

Not only was the fleet getting larger but so were the buses themselves. Eight feet wide buses, an increase of six inches, first appeared in the Midland Red fleet in 1948. Then, in 1950, single-deckers were allowed to be 30ft long and double-deckers 27ft 6in. The closing vehicles of the 500 early postwar single-deckers were built to the new length, enabling an extra row of seats, and the remainder were subsequently extended. Following on from these vehicles were some 30-footers which were to dual-purpose specification, ie having a quality of seating ideal for longer distance stage services but suitable for express work when the coach fleet was under pressure.

BMMO turned its attention to reducing vehicle weight and, in the mid-1950s, produced a large number of very light integral single-deckers. The standard double-decker of the same era, the D7, retained a chassis but also featured lightweight bodywork. The last true 'heavyweights' to enter Midland Red service were 100 Leyland double-deckers, delivered in 1952-3 to meet urgent fleet needs, and 75 BMMO coaches built in 1953-4.

The next batch of coaches, of which production commenced in 1959, was the famous C5 design. Its main claim to fame was the turbocharged CM5T variants which introduced motorway express services to Britain and gave the company immense operational and technical prestige. But more was to come. The chassisless concept was extended to double-deckers with the introduction of the D9 type, which incorporated a host of new and often advanced features. Technical expertise reached its peak in 1960, however, when the mechanical features of the D9 were incorporated into an underfloor-engined double-decker, the D10. BMMO astounded the manufacturers who felt such a machine was not practicable as the floor level would become too high to allow a double-deck body. The D10 was not unsuccessful but its now obvious suitability for one-man operation was not foreseen at the time. Thus only two were built and production continued of the simpler D9 front-engined design.

The programme of new garages and extensions to cope with the enlarging fleet has already been mentioned. There were also some other significant building developments. A handsome building conveniently adjacent to Carlyle works was acquired, named 'Midland House', and became the registered offices of the company in 1953. The Carlyle Road central works were themselves being extensively rebuilt and were proudly reopened the following year. In the late 1950s the Birmingham Digbeth garage was reconstructed to include a modern coach station although latterly, despite further improvements, the combination of passenger circulation and vehicle maintenance facilities under one roof has been criticised. Lastly there was the opening of the Bull Ring Bus Station in 1963 which brought together all the company's Birmingham services (except the Dudley Road group jointly operated with Birmingham City

Transport) into one central terminus for the first time. This was obviously a great improvement over the previous widely scattered street termini. The new bus station was entirely undercover although again this has latterly brought complaints regarding fumes.

One-man operation of buses had begun, using S14 type single-deckers, in 1956 as an answer to rising costs and the difficulty in recruiting platform staff. The bus industry was notoriously poorly paid and recruitment on both platform and engineering sides became steadily more difficult. Rising costs led to fare increases which led in turn to diminishing numbers of passengers who found private motoring an effective answer to higher fares and the resultant service cuts. This was hardly the right climate to correct the pay problem, at a time when other industries were rewarding their employees more generously. The company was running into trouble.

The gradual spread of one-man operation, and its accompanying enhanced rates of pay, reduced the staff problems slightly on the platform side. However the then healthy motor industry tempted away many skilled engineers during the 1960s. Increasing numbers of Leyland Leopards and Daimler Fleetlines supplemented the falling output of new vehicles from Carlyle Works. Some garages experienced chronic shortages of engineering staff and reliability fell on those buses which were blessed with drivers. A number of vehicles were hired with drivers, a costly manoeuvre to stem the loss of passengers forced away by unreliable services.

Construction of new vehicles at Carlyle Road eventually fell to an uneconomic level and the last BMMO-produced bus entered service in 1970, only 10 years after the high point of BMMO expertise marked by the D10. Mr Sinclair had retired at the end of 1966 although, after the D10, new BMMO products were rather an anticlimax. Thirty-six feet long single-deckers had been permissible from 1961 and the first model to the new length retained the traditional 8litre engine and 'crash' gearbox. This was fortunately soon superseded by designs which incorporated the 10.5litre engine and semi-automatic gearbox of the D9. A new motorway coach fleet was built to the revised dimensions. So the story of BMMO as a manufacturer ends and one wonders what happened to all that knowledge and experience of vehicle design and building.

This really was the end of an era because the BET had decided to sell its interests in the bus industry to the state, taking effect in March 1968. These interests were merged with existing state bus operations to form the National Bus Company. The NBC believed in much more central control than the BET and so the company lost much of its individuality. Personnel changed too and the

Below: The outbreak of war in 1939 saw the commandeering by the military of a considerable number of older vehicles and a big increase in demand for factory services. The war also brought an end to long-distance coach services for the duration to conserve fuel. The oldest coaches still owned, the RR family, were loaned to Potteries Motor Traction from 1940 and only two ever re-entered BMMO service. The LRR coaches were relegated to 34-seat buses and AHA 596 is seen, after conversion, in Union Road, Nottingham, during August 1940. Note the masked headlamps and white marker paint for use in the blackout. The LRRs became particularly associated with Leamington garage where services from Coventry, already under pressure from factory traffic, were overwhelmed after the November 1940 blitz devastation by passengers leaving the city each night and endeavouring to return the following morning. The staff position was so bad, with so many men in the forces, that for some months a bus had to leave Swadlincote garage at 4am, travelling via Coalville and Leicester, collecting those crews that could be spared, for duties at Rugby and Leamington. *G. H. F. Atkins*

Bottom: There was obviously even less requirement for touring coaches, and the 25 OLR convertible normal-control vehicles were extensively rebuilt into forward control, fixed-roof 34-seat service buses. AHA 632 is seen at Evesham in postwar years. The LRRs and OLRs remained in bus form and were withdrawn around 1951-2. *G. H. Stone*

succession of general managers which followed Mr Sinclair's departure did not assist continuity. These factors combined to make Midland Red from 1970 a very different company to that of 10 years earlier.

Right: The Ministry of Supply also allocated to BMMO six of these AEC Regents with Brush bodies. They were originally intended for Coventry Corporation and one would have thought that their intended operator's needs were more pressing, in view of the blitz damage in that city. Their AEC 7.7litre engines were, however, familiar to BMMO, being fitted also in the DON class. Midland Red fortunately no longer had a garage in Coventry and, indeed throughout the system, managed to avoid serious damage from the Luftwaffe. Incendiary bombs fell through the roofs of a number of garages, but serious fires were prevented by the prompt action of staff. Damage to buses was minimised by the practice of overnight parking away from garages. *AEC*

Below: The wartime double-deckers, built by outside manufacturers, were highly non-standard but much needed. Most carried austerity bodies but three of the Leyland TD7 Titans received in 1942 carried all-metal Northern Counties bodies of peacetime design. One, GHA 792, is seen at Wolverhampton Station. The Leyland engines were eventually replaced by BMMO units. *R. T. Wilson*

Below right: The bulk of the wartime intake consisted of Guy Arabs and Daimler CWA6s, with Gardner 5LW and AEC 7.7litre engines respectively, carrying austerity bodies. Daimler GHA 945 with Duple body was typical. *Alan B. Cross*

Left: Even Northern Counties bodies became more utilitarian but retained rounded window corners. 1945 Guy Arab II HHA 84 is seen at Leicester. *Roy Marshall*

Below left: The postwar look begins to evolve. FEDD EHA 299 with the full-width bonnet, concealed radiator, and rebuilt upper deck that was fitted in 1942. The bus reverted to exposed radiator when the body was rebuilt in 1951.

Bottom left: The 1945 prototype double-decker, subsequently classified the D1. The concealed radiator, four-bay construction and sliding ventilators within fully-radiused windows had all been seen before elsewhere but not in one vehicle. HHA 1 (nicknamed 'Harry-One' by some) was a classic, years ahead of its time, and looked quite staggering compared to the utility vehicles then entering service. It was fitted with electrically operated platform doors in 1949 to test their feasibility and continued in service until 1961. *Midland Red*

Below: Even more remarkable were the underfloor-engined prototypes, rebuilt from the prewar rear-engined experimentals. The first to be rebuilt, and the most bizarre in appearance, was BHA 1 which was reconstructed in 1941. It was subsequently typecoded S1, and is seen here at Bearwood carrying post-1944 fleet number 1591. *S. E. Letts*

Above left: CHA 1-3 became prototypes S2 to S4. The S3, fleet No 1943, is seen at Acocks Green, Birmingham, shortly after the war. This bus was known as 'Charlie Two' because of its registration. *Michael Rooum*

Left: The 100 AEC Regent IIs were classified AD2 — the A prefix denoting the AEC parentage of the non-BMMO chassis. The 50 Brush bodied examples arrived in 1948; No 3125 is seen here at Leicester in October 1950. *G. H. F. Atkins*

Below: A further prototype, entirely new and of integral (chassisless) construction, entered service in 1946 as type S5. By the time the first 100 production vehicles, type S6, entered service in 1946-7, the proportions had been refined to this neat style. Mr Sinclair reverted to separate chassis and body construction for the time being. The body contract was shared between Brush and Metro-Cammell. No 3024 was bodied by the latter — it was possible to differentiate between the two. *Midland Red*

Left: The company's coach fleet was somewhat depleted when operations were resumed at the end of the war, comprising only the 50 SLRs and 25 ONCs. The SLRs were extensively refitted with new grilles and trim, which eliminated all trace of their 1930s 'art deco' heritage. They were also completely reupholstered and repainted in the smart postwar red and black coaching livery. The thirsty petrol engines were dispensed with to be replaced, rather surprisingly, by Leyland E181 diesels. There was apparently insufficient room between the chassis sidemembers to fit BMMO diesel engines. The facelifted SLRs were then able to continue in service until 1955. No 2000 presents a splendid profile at Leicester in August 1953. Many of these went for further use abroad. *G. H. F. Atkins*

Below left: Attractive early postwar route map, produced in colour, with a drawing of the D1 carrying a D5 registration number. Note the reference to free enterprise buses and also to the 'Friendly Midland Red' — a slogan which survived for many, many years until, presumably, the quantity of unfriendly staff made it an embarrassment.

Bottom left: Eight-feet wide buses were introduced as soon as possible after regulations were relaxed. The first type was the appropriately designated S8, built in 1948-9 with Metro-Cammell bodies, followed in 1949-50 by the Brush-bodied S9. Each class was 100 strong. S9 No 3392 awaits custom in Dudley Street, Birmingham, on the site of today's bus station. *R. A. Mills*

Right: One S9 was radically different, incorporating a new front end with electrically operated folding doors at the entrance in lieu of the hinged door at the front of the saloon. The appearance of No 3441 now looks rather orthodox but much was made of its trans-Atlantic styling when it first appeared in 1950 — Mr Sinclair had recently visited the United States. Prototypes around this time were usually graced or burdened by liberal quantities of brightwork. The scene is Leicester where No 3441 spent nearly all its life. *J. P. Addenbrooke*

Below: The C1 class of underfloor-engined coaches with Duple bodies entered service for the 1949 season and were years ahead of their half-cab or normal-control competitors. The advanced styling enabled these coaches to remain in service until 1965 without undue embarrassment. A London view of No 3343. *A. Hustwitt*

Left: Twelve more similar coaches followed in 1950. These were the C2 class, intended for Coach Cruises (Midland Red's up-market term for Extended Tours), and seating 26 compared to the 30 of the C1. Most were up-seated upon receipt of new and larger tour coaches in 1954 but three survived for those Coach Cruises which required short and narrow vehicles. No 3348 is seen at Cheltenham in June 1965. *Maurice Collignon*

Below left: Midland Red had to wait until 1950 for most of its AD2 buses with Metro-Cammell bodies, giving some idea of the delivery delays after the war. Detail differences could be discerned between these and their Brush-bodied brethren, notably the increased number of opening windows. No 3189 loads at Banbury in the early 1950s. *Alan B. Cross*

Below: The shortage of vehicles forced the company to depart from its standard by the purchase of 20 'off-the-peg' Guy Arabs. A totally Wolverhampton product, they carried Park Royal-design bodies built under licence by Guy and were powered by 10.35litre Meadows 6DC engines. They were mighty machines, and contemptuously overcame the hilly routes served by Dudley garage, to which the class was allocated. On a quiet Sunday morning, the bellowing exhaust note could carry to the ears of a listener a good mile away. The bodies were, however, spartan, and the single-skin roof and sides, and the absence of heaters subjected passengers and crews to extremes of temperature according to season. Unfortunately the Meadows engines provided troublesome to maintain and their replacement in 1952 by BMMO 'K'-type engines from withdrawn prewar stock resulted in a much more staid performance. Most of these Guys, typecoded GD6 in the BMMO system, were withdrawn in 1962. *Roy Marshall*

Above: The first standard BMMO postwar double-deckers began to enter service in 1949. This was the D5 class with Brush bodies built to the new 8ft width. No 3553 is typical of the first hundred and awaits its departure time from Lower Parade, Sutton Coldfield. It is obviously very new and has not yet been fitted with the vents above the front upper deck windows which emphasised the slightly 'sad' appearance of AD2 and D5 buses. *R. T. Wilson*

Right: Another 200 single-deckers were built in 1949-51, of which the majority were of Type S10. Metro-Cammell bodied 3600 prepares to leave Station Street, Birmingham, on the then rare and now defunct 413 service to Symonds Yat. The 200 also included the solitary S11, which featured independent front wheel suspension, whilst the last 44 took advantage of the newly permitted length on two axles of 30ft and were designated S12. This enabled 44 seats to be fitted, an increase of four. *Michael Rooum*

Below right: The first 30-footer was, however, the prototype S13 which was on the road on the first day of the relaxed regulations — 1 June 1950. As usual, BMMO did not hang about! No 3694 apears to need all of its 44 seats as it departs from Navigation Street, Birmingham. Brush bodied buses for Midland Red featured this improved style of ventilator by this time. *R. A. Mills*

Below: Never averse to increasing the capacity of its buses, the company had all of its early postwar single-deck fleet lengthened to nearly 30ft to gain that extra row of four seats. Lengthened Metro-Cammell bodied S10 No 3620 receives attention from an Essex washer at Worcester in the mid-1950s. *Midland Red*

Above: The second 100 D5s, built between 1950 and 1952, had electrically operated platform doors — another example of the company standardising whilst others were still experimenting. This modified design was coded D5B. No 3796 at Southgate Street, Leicester, in September 1951. *G. H. F. Atkins*

Above: Despite all these new vehicles, the postwar travel boom meant limited inroads into the ranks of prewar stock. Many prewar buses were extensively rehabilitated to prolong their lives. The first rebuilds were a number of 1934-5 CON and DON models which received new all-metal sides of severe appearance. DON 1713 at Leicester in 1950. *R. A. Mills*

Below: A large number of CON, DON and SON bodies were revitalised by Nudd Bros & Lockyer of Kegworth between 1949 and 1951. The rebuilds could be recognised by their rubber mounted windows with plain, sliding vents which robbed the buses of some character and almost all their style. Numerically one of the oldest buses to be rebuilt, 1503, is seen on a temporary parking ground off Dudley Street, Birmingham. *Alan B. Cross*

Below: All the Brush-bodied FEDDs were attended to between 1949 and 1951, in almost every case the work being carried out by Aero & Engineering (Merseyside) Ltd, Hooton. The last FEDD numerically, No 2381, is seen near the end of its life, at Bearwood Bus Station. *Alan D. Broughall*

Left: In some cases only the lower deck was treated. A passing Midland Red enthusiast would have been delighted to be offered the opportunity to travel to the Malverns by FEDD in August 1958. This was Bank Holiday Monday and No 2346 is loading in Hinckley Street, Birmingham, to prevent the crowds and attendant buses from blocking the then important Station Street terminus. *F. W. York*

Above right: The wartime buses were also found to be in need of attention due to the unavoidable use of substandard timber. One Guy and one Daimler were rebuilt by Carlyle in 1949 as prototypes. The remaining Daimlers were despatched to Willowbrook in 1950-1 to return in the manner exemplified by No 2547. It stands in the Bull Ring, Birmingham — an area itself altered beyond recognition. Note that the rebuilds of wartime buses included curious built-up front wings and postwar style destination boxes. The rehabilitation of these inferior wartime bodies was only partially successful — they rattled their way out of the fleet around 1955-6. *Alan B. Cross*

Right: Most of the Guys were attended to by Brush in 1950-1. Here, No 2550 loads at Leicester in October 1950. *G. H. F. Atkins*

Below: The metal framed Northern Counties-bodied Guys required little attention and merely received a facelift. The conductor of No 2588 checks his watch whilst the sky remains angry after the recent thunderstorm; St Margaret's Bus Station, Leicester, in August 1952. *G. H. F. Atkins*

Above: The final rehabilitation programme, undertaken at Hooton in 1951-2, embraced the remaining unrebuilt 1934-5 CONs and DONs, and many 1936 SONs. Thus DON 1715 was already 17 years old when it received its second lease of life. Alongside in this October 1953 view at Leicester is a production S13, No 3954, with Nudd Bros body. *G. H. F. Atkins*

Below: Nearly all the production S13s were to dual purpose bus/coach specification, and received the red and black coach livery in 1956. No 3892, built in 1952 with Brush body, is seen at Park Row, Nottingham during July 1956. Most of the S13s were withdrawn in 1966. *G. H. F. Atkins*

Above: BMMO turned out this lightweight, chassisless, single-decker in 1951, classified the LA (Light Alloy). By 1960 it was out of use but in its time it ran with an experimental BMMO 10.5litre engine, then with a Leyland 5.75litre, and finally with the BMMO 8litre. The queue in Navigation Street, Birmingham, only has eyes for the young lady but it is the older man with the pipe that has her attention. *Roy Marshall*

Right: The lightweight D7 double-decker first appeared in 1953 and by 1957 there were 350 of them, making the D7 the most numerous BMMO type of all. Metro-Cammell built the bodies, and the appearance of No 4085, at Southgate Street, Leicester, in October 1953, benefits from the black wings and gold lining. The livery had been simplified to unrelieved red by the time the last examples appeared. *G. H. F. Atkins*

Above: One hundred Leyland PD2 Titans, bodied by Leyland itself, supplemented Midland Red's own production and formed the LD8 class. The first of the contract, No 3978, was a Leyland exhibit at the 1952 Commercial Motor Show. The wide bonnet design, devised to meet BMMO standards of appearance, was adopted by Leyland for a number of years. *Leyland*

DIGBETH GARAGE.

Above left: Digbeth garage received a large number of LD8s which proved well suited to the long, frequently rural and fastly timed routes operated from there. These were fine looking machines when new but their appearance was ruined by unsympathetic treatment when spray painting was introduced. The important Bull Ring terminus in Birmingham was first used in February 1914 when BMMO introduced the Birmingham-Coventry service. No 4020 is about to leave the Bull Ring with a good load for Coventry. The LD8s were withdrawn between 1965 and 1967, and a small number found new homes. *Alan B. Cross*

Left: Digbeth garage prior to the rebuilding in the 1950s.

Left: A picture which successfully captures the atmosphere of travelling by road in the 1950s. The white-coated driver pilots No 4193, one of 63 C3 class coaches with Willowbrook 37-seat bodies built in 1954, through Bignell's Corner on the A1. Behind is No 2008, one of the SLRs replaced by the C3s.
A. Hustwitt

Below left: There were also 12 new extended tour coaches, originally seating 32, which formed the C4 class. The first, No 4242, was built in 1953 with a Carlyle body and acted as prototype for the C3 and C4 types. The remaining 11 were built the following year with Alexander bodies. The C4s were instantly identifiable by the extra glazing above the side windows to improve observation. No 4247 is seen, shortly before withdrawal, on ordinary coach duties at Cheltenham in May 1966. *Maurice Collignon*

Above right: The lightweight S14 model was significant in a number of ways, in particular marking the general adoption by BMMO of chassisless construction and the return to quantity body production at Carlyle Road Works. The prototype, No 4178, loads in Nottingham during October 1955 — this was one of several S14s originally fitted with Hobbs automatic transmission instead of the usual constant-mesh gearbox. *G. H. F. Atkins*

Right: One-man operated vehicles were introduced in 1956, initially using S14s with modified cabs. Suitably equipped 1958 S14 No 4692 is seen at Banbury in May 1963. The S14s only weighed a little over five tons and had single rear wheels.
Alan D. Broughall

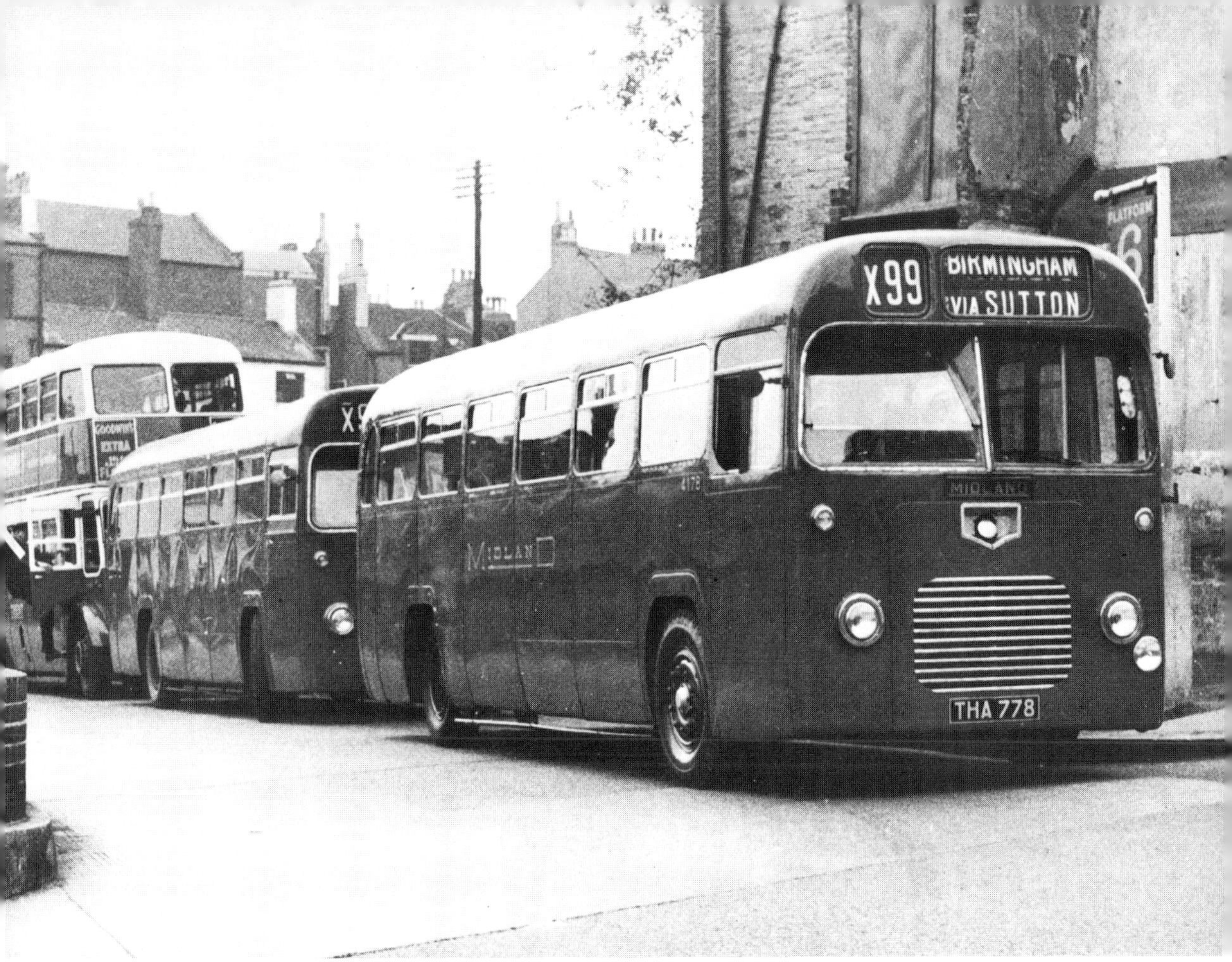
X99
BIRMINGHAM
VIA SUTTON
PLATFORM
6
MIDLAND
THA 778

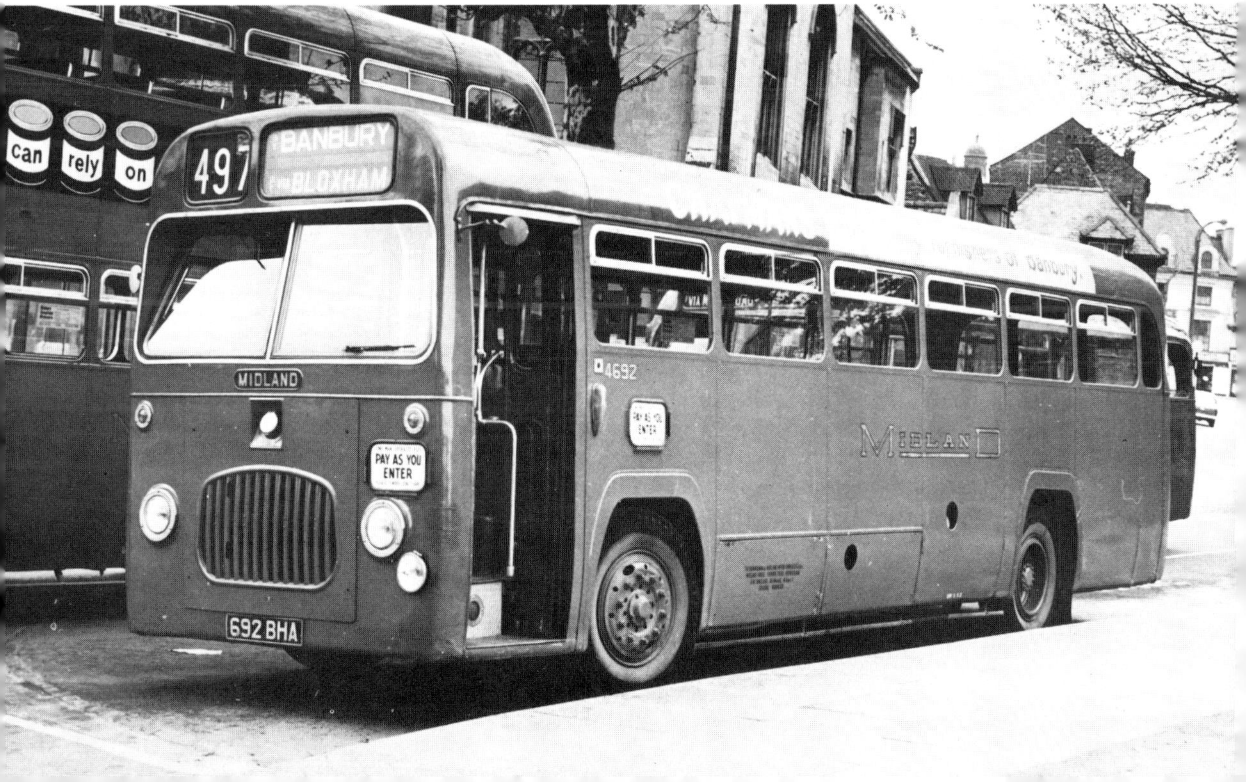
can
rely
on
497
BANBURY
BLOXHAM
MIDLAND
4692
PAY AS YOU ENTER
692 BHA

Above: The company built 50 further dual-purpose vehicles in 1957. This was the S15 class, which was a beefed-up version of the S14, including a reversion to twin rear wheels. The most obvious recognition points were the hopper ventilators and, until relegation to ordinary work, the red and black coach livery. Two S15s travelling in opposite directions on the infrequent X73 Birmingham-Cheltenham service meet at Worcester Bus Station in June 1961. Four S15s were loaned to other BET subsidiaries in 1957/8 when it seemed possible that BMMO was considering the production of vehicles for associated companies again. *C. J. Davis*

Right: Whilst the standard BMMO bus interior could be quite spartan in appearance, that of the S15 was decidedly cosy. *Midland Red*

Above: Three S8s received S15 front ends, including power doors, in 1957-8. They were also re-upholstered so 3237 would have proved sufficiently comfortable for the long X96 Northampton to Shrewsbury service in June 1962. This service, around 100 miles in length with approximately 150 fare stages, called into Digbeth Coach Station, seen in the background, rather than stopping outside.
Maurice Norton

Left: No 4722 was the 1958 prototype of a chassisless new coach, the C5, based on S15 running units. Gone were the flowing lines and centre entrance of its predecessors — the C5 marked a major change in coach design. Production vehicles entered service the following year.
Mark Alexander

Above: The share capital of Kemp & Shaw Ltd of Leicester had been acquired in 1955 but the buses did not enter the Midland Red fleet until 1 January 1959, when Kemp & Shaw was liquidated. A month later, another Leicestershire operator was acquired, H. Boyer and Son of Rothley. Their vehicles also entered the fleet — the retention of non-standard buses from acquired operators was an exceedingly rare event. Kemp & Shaw operated a quartet of early postwar Guy Arabs with Northern Counties bodies. The future Midland Red No 4840 awaits repainting at Carlyle Works in 1959. The C2 alongside, No 3351, was one of three still used on extended tours and facelifted that year. *G. H. Stone*

Below: Kemp & Shaw contributed two 1949 Guy Arab IIIs with Barnard bodies which reintroduced vertical engined vehicles to the single-deck fleet and looked archaic as a consequence. The future No 4842 is seen in July 1953 when Kemp & Shaw was still independent. *Roy Marshall*

Left: The only true 'lowbridge' (ie side gangway) bus to be operated by Midland Red was this 1950 Leyland-bodied Leyland PD2 ex-Kemp & Shaw. Staff discuss a matter of mutual interest in front of an immaculate No 4844 at St Margaret's, Leicester, in August 1961. Despite its inconvenient interior layout, No 4844 ran until 1967. *Alan D. Broughall*

Below: Two more secondhand Leyland-bodied Leylands: ex-Kemp & Shaw Titan No 4845 and ex-Boyer Royal Tiger No 4848, both dating from 1952, meet at St Margaret's in September 1965. *Maurice Collignon*

Bottom: Boyer contributed two rare Sentinels. No 4847 was a 1951 STC6 model with Sentinel's own 44-seat body which was withdrawn in 1961. *G. H. F. Atkins*

Top: One of the proudest days in the company's history was Monday 2 November 1959, when Britain's first motorway was opened. Midland Red, with customary foresight, had obtained the necessary road service licences and was thus able to bring in an express facility on the very first day. Moreover a new fleet of turbocharged coaches was introduced, capable of 80mph without losing breath. This C5 variant was designated CM5T — the T suffix indicated the provision of a toilet. Nos 4805 and 4809 leave Digbeth Coach Station on that first day. *Ian Allan Library*

Above: The motorway coaches were soon fitted with twin headlamps, a status symbol on private cars at the time, to improve the range of the dipped beam. Other operators commenced express services via the motorway in due course, although the honours of pioneering today's National Express network must remain with Midland Red. Here, at London's Victoria Coach Station in January 1965, alongside a Bristol RE of United Counties, No 4801 waits to return to Birmingham. *F. W. York*

Above: The handsome D9 model went into production in 1960 and well over 300 were on the road by the time the last entered service six years later. Many S14 features were present, including chassisless construction, rubber suspension and Carlyle-built body. There was also the first standard installation of the BMMO 10.5litre engine, and a semi-automatic gearbox which, at last, took the hard work out of gearchanging. Built to 30ft length, the D9s would seat 72 passengers. No 4880 was one of many fitted with illuminated advertisement panels, in this case promoting the Company's motorway express services.
D. D. Kirk

Left: Hot on the heels of the D9s came the revolutionary D10s, the only underfloor-engined double-deckers to enter service in Great Britain until Volvo's excursion into this field in 1982. Despite the position of the engine, the D10 had adequate headroom in both decks. The first D10, No 4943, is seen at Bradford Place, Walsall, in the company of one of Walsall Corporation's peculiar short length Daimler Fleetlines. *Maurice Collignon*

Below left: The second D10 featured a rear exit and additional staircase, dubious modifications which reduced the seating capacity from the 78 passengers of the first D10 to only 65. No 4944 is seen at Dudley in September 1962, shortly before the vehicle was converted to single door and staircase. The conductor has an ironic expression on his face — possibly complaining in true Black Country style of the need to chase reluctant farepayers around the bus via the two staircases! *Maurice Norton*

Above: A fleet of new extended tour coaches was produced for the 1962 season by the surprise rebodying of 16 C3 chassis with Plaxton Panorama 36-seat bodies to form class CL3. The choice of an off-white livery was an even bigger upset but, fortunately, traditional red and black was soon substituted. *Plaxtons*

Right: Three C2s were also rebodied for those tours which required coaches of small dimensions. These received Plaxton Embassy 26-seat bodies and CL2 No 3346 is seen at Digbeth in September 1965 after repainting in 'proper' livery. The CL2 and CL3 types were withdrawn in 1971. *Maurice Collignon*

Below right: The difficulty in obtaining staff caused the hiring of vehicles with drivers from G & G Coaches of Leamington for a number of years. Ex-Devon General AEC Regent III (RT type) HTT 332, with Weymann body, loads at Pool Meadow, Coventry.
Alan D. Broughall

Above: Production of the S14 had ceased at the end of 1958, upon the withdrawal of the last prewar single-deckers. The early postwar fleet was now becoming due for replacement, so the company planned to resume manufacture of the S14 and S15 in 1962. Indeed, 48 of the latter were produced that year but BMMO then went ahead with 50 of its new 36ft long S16 model, of which a prototype had appeared early in 1962, soon after the regulations had been relaxed. The new giants seated 52 and featured a much wider entrance door. It was at this time that Carlyle Road Works began to have difficulty in producing sufficient bodies. Many partly completed buses were despatched therefore to Plaxton or Willowbrook for finishing. S16 No 5130, seen at Leicester in July 1963, had a body completed by Plaxton. *Alan D. Broughall*

Below: 100 Leyland PSU3 Leopards with Willowbrook or Weymann bodies to the new length were received in 1962-3, forming the LS18 class. Twenty of the Willowbrooks were to dual purpose specification and looked extremely smart in red and black. No 5178 awaits further work from Shrewsbury garage in July 1963. These powerful buses with semi-automatic gearboxes were willing workhorses and were not withdrawn until the late 1970s, the final examples finishing in 1980. *Maurice Collignon*

MIDLAND
L8
SOUTH WIGSTON
WIGSTON MAGNA
5284 HA
MIDLAND
L20
MELTON ROAD
XHA 462
MIDLAND
38
6370 HA

MIDLAND
706
6302 HA
TOWN HALL
Come Co-operative
24
FA 7959

Left: 50 Daimler Fleetlines with Alexander 77-seat bodies were also received in 1963 to round off a year in which severe inroads were made into the ranks of early postwar buses. The Fleetlines were, of course, the first rear-engined buses in the fleet since the prewar experimentals. DD11 No 5284 awaits departure at St Margaret's, Leicester, in June 1967, alongside D7 No 4462 and D9 No 5370. *G. H. F. Atkins*

Below left: D9s continued to emerge from Carlyle Works. No 5302 contrasts with a wartime Guy with austerity pattern Weymann body that still remained in service with Burton Corporation. *Robert F. Mack*

Right: The S16 was a lacklustre design, with the small BMMO 8litre engine coupled to the old constant-mesh gearbox. It was joined later in 1963 by the S17 which incorporated the 10.5litre engine and semi-automatic gearbox first combined in the D9. A large number of S17s were turned out by 1966, only one further batch of S16s being produced, in 1964. S17 No 5549 proceeds along Corporation Street, Birmingham, in November 1973. *MRK*

Below: Another Leicester area independent, Brown's Blue of Markfield, was acquired in March 1963. This time no vehicles entered BMMO service but the garage was used until 1968. This ex-London Transport Daimler CWA6, seen alongside D5B No 3872 in July 1953, had been withdrawn long before the takeover. *Roy Marshall*

Above: A new motorway coach to take advantage of the relaxed dimensions, the CM6T, entered service in 1963. No 5295 initially employed a C5 windscreen but was restyled as shown later in the year. *Midland Red*

Right: The 29 production motorway coaches did not appear until 1965/6 and looked rather different. This view at London's Victoria Coach Station in August 1966 is unusual as it shows No 5670, one of the CM6 toiletless coaches intended for the Birmingham to Worcester motorway service. These coaches clocked up impressive mileages but had short lives, being withdrawn in 1972-4 when certain spares became impossible to obtain. *Maurice Collignon*

Below right: The company now began to standardise on Leyland Leopards for coach work. Fifty were purchased in 1965, 49 with Duple bodies (Type LC7) whilst the odd man out was a short Leopard with Plaxton body for extended tours (Type LC8). LC7 No 5800 loads at London Victoria in September 1965. *G. H. F. Atkins*

Below: Fifteen more short (31ft) Leopards with Plaxton bodies were received in 1966 for extended tours. This was the LC9 class which originally seated 36, subsequently increased by four. No 5827, seen on a tour of Devon and Cornwall in June 1972, carries the red and maroon livery favoured from May 1967 for coaches and semi-coaches. The intake of motorway coaches and Leopards in 1965-6 enabled all remaining C1s, the unrebodied C2s and C3s, and the C4s to be withdrawn. Having achieved this modernisation a shorter life for coaches was subsequently maintained.
Alan D. Broughall

Above: Ten Leyland Leopard semi-coaches with Willowbrook 49-seat bodies entered service early in 1967, forming the LS20 class (the S19 was an experimental BMMO model based on the S17). The driver of No 5839, seen at Coventry in March 1967, was a familiar sight on services from Digbeth garage — always immaculate in his bow tie and looking as though he had been diverted at the last minute from an important private hire requiring evening dress.
Maurice Collignon

Above: Production of BMMO double-deckers had ceased in 1966 with D9 No 5445. To fill the gap, 149 Alexander-bodied Daimler Fleetlines were put into service as Class DD12 between 1966 and 1968. These had a somewhat uninspired style of fleetname as shown by No 6120 at Malvern Wells terminus in July 1968. The company was about to enter a very muddled period regarding fleet name and lettering styles. *Maurice Collignon*

Right: Midland Red, as part of the BET Federation, joined the chorus of protests at the threat of nationalisation presented by Minister of Transport Barbara Castle in October 1967. D9 No 4868, covered in private enterprise slogans, was of course already part state-owned as the railways, who owned a large share in the company, had been nationalised in 1948. BET sold out to the state only a month after this photograph was taken, paving the way for the National Bus Company. *Midland Red*

Left: The last BMMO vehicles were a family of single-deckers built to varying standards of seating comfort. The 30 S21 models built in 1967 were described as semicoaches and thus appeared with black or, on later examples, maroon roofs. No 5855 is seen at Mount Street, Nottingham, in August 1967. *G. H. F. Atkins*

Below left: The 37 S22 vehicles built in 1968 fell into the dual-purpose category and, like all such vehicles by this time, were painted entirely red. The first of the series, No 5879, is seen at Shrewsbury Bus Station in September 1972. *MRK*

Below: The final BMMO production consisted of 76 S23 service buses, the last to be built entirely at Carlyle Road being No 5941, entering service in January 1970. This was followed later in the year by Plaxton-finished 5991, the very last BMMO of all. No 5941 is surrounded here at Wigston garage in March 1979 by non-BMMO vehicles. The last BMMO buses to run in normal service were the four S23s taken out of use at the end of February 1981. Their demise was hastened by service cuts and the cost and difficulty of providing spares for a diminishing number of vehicles. *MRK*

Below: The 1969 batch of 15 Leopards for extended tour work were the first to be graced by Plaxton Panorama Elite coachwork and also introduced the Leyland 0680 engine to the fleet — previous Leopards having 0600 engines. The new series took the typecode LC10. No 6143 turns right from Digbeth into Rea Street to gain access to Birmingham's Coach Station in July 1972. Further short length Leyland PSU4 Leopards were added to stock between 1971 and 1973. *Maurice Collignon*

Bottom: The 30 Leopards received in 1970 reverted to the PSU3 36ft long model and also this earlier style of Plaxton coachwork. LC11 No 6228 leads an impressive line of seven Leopards on a private charter in Colmore Row, Birmingham, in May 1972. *MRK*

Top: A total of 70 Alexander-bodied Daimler Fleetlines entered service in 1969. These DD13s looked generally similar to the earlier Fleetlines but the 6LX engine was succeeded by the more powerful 6LXB, whilst the bodies featured a separate centre exit to speed unloading. No 6176 leaves St Margaret's Bus Station in September 1969. A further 33 DD13s of generally similar appearance were received in 1970/1. The subsequent decision to cease purchasing double-deckers meant that these Fleetlines worked hard throughout lives that were longer than might have been expected. *G. H. F. Atkins*

Above: Surprise purchases in 1970 were five Leyland L1 Leopards which had begun life in 1960 with Sheffield Joint Committee's 'C' fleet. Weymann Fanfare 41-seat bodies were fitted. These coaches were used by Midland Red as service buses and it was suggested that they might be the first of a string of secondhand purchases to assist in the removal of ageing BMMO stock. This proved not to be and, indeed, the Sheffield Leopards themselves were withdrawn the following year. No 6256 is seen at Edgbaston Street, Birmingham, during August 1970 en route to Walsall. The entrance door was hand-operated by the driver with a large lever similar, and sited adjacent, to the handbrake. Thus an unfamiliar driver, stopping on a hill and applying the 'handbrake', would be disconcerted to discover the door opening and the bus rolling backwards! *Maurice Collignon*

MAP to Oblivion

An early effect of National Bus Company management was the absorption of Stratford-upon-Avon Blue Motors with effect from 1 January 1971. Stratford Blue had been a Midland Red subsidiary since 1935 but its small fleet of, largely, Leylands did not give any obvious indication of this. The BET appeared to favour the retention of small companies which gave managers useful experience before moving on to larger undertakings. The existence of these small companies would not help the forthcoming NBC corporate image policy and so Stratford Blue had to go.

The next outward sign of NBC management was the adoption of a white 'National' coach livery for all subsidiaries, including Midland Red. The idea of the single livery was to bring home to the general public the existence of a national coach network. The full benefit of the corporate coach livery and the express network concept was not to be fully realised until after the 1980 Transport Act when the white coaches were threatened on their best routes by the de-regulated private sector. Rigorous promotion of the nationwide white express coaches, coupled with an aggressive fares policy, not only minimised the effect of the relatively piecemeal private operations but also increased carryings! The imposition of the corporate livery had carried a heavy price for operators like Midland Red, however. The extensive goodwill built up by the company was largely swept aside as tours and excursions clients who traditionally travelled Midland Red compared the National offerings with those of private operators. Many former clients must have been deterred from National tours by the sight of the white express coaches which became grubby after the slightest shower.

NBC corporate livery also spread to the bus fleet. Initially NBC subsidiaries who traditionally painted their vehicles red were required to choose one of two shades of that colour. Midland Red chose the lighter but even that was of a darker, duller hue than the traditional. Soon afterwards this was superseded by poppy red which became standard from the autumn of 1972. This shade was much brighter but, although it looked fresh particularly when combined with white relief, an ex-paintshops example never looked as striking as the traditional red. The poppy red was combined with corporate image lettering in the modern idiom which, whilst clear, lacked class and style.

Following the cessation of BMMO vehicle production in 1970, Leyland Leopards were received in large numbers in bus, dual-purpose and coach forms. More unusual, however, was the large number of Ford saloons taken between 1970 and 1974 to modernise the ageing rural fleet. From 1973, NBC subsidiaries were required to take Leyland Nationals to meet their service bus requirements. Thus Midland Red had not only ceased to build its own buses but now could no longer choose their successors! Leyland Leopards were now only taken in dual-purpose and coach forms. From 1976, dual-purpose Leopards ceased to use a bus shell but assumed the more glamorous guise of a coach design.

It was decreed in September 1975 that Midland Red was not to have any more double-deckers, indeed the last such vehicles received new, apart from two ordered by an independent and delivered direct to the company, had been Daimler Fleetlines in 1971.

Arguably the most traumatic event during this period was the sale of the Birmingham and Black Country services to the West Midlands Passenger Transport Executive with effect from December 1973. The PTE was required under the 1968 Transport Act to have control of all services within its area and, as an agency arrangement could not be agreed, the only alternative was for the PTE to buy the company services. The deal included the transfer of 413 buses, six garages and a large number of experienced platform, engineering and office staff to the Executive. Company buses were still to be seen in quantity in Birmingham, however, on services operating to points outside what became West Midlands County in April 1974. Rather curiously however Midland Red seemed anxious to convert lucrative stopping services, with revenue guaranteed by the PTE, into limited or non-stop facilities that did not attract such support.

The company was left with an operating territory with a distinctly rural emphasis. Unfortunately support for rural services rested with county councils whose attitudes to public transport were to vary widely. In the meantime, the £3.6million received from the West Midlands was earmarked for investment, to give the company a stronger base for the future, rather than for the short term expedient of subsidising existing operations. A number of independent firms was taken over around this time, notably Green Bus of Rugeley (in 1973), Harper Brothers of Heath Hayes (in 1974) and the bus operations of the Shropshire Omnibus Association Ltd. This latter manoeuvre, in 1978, enabled Midland Red entirely to restructure services in the Telford and Wellington areas. No buses were taken over in the last mentioned purchase and Midland Red allocated a fleet of new Leyland Nationals to Wellington garage to operate the new network. The company also invested in a new garage at Cannock, to handle the increased operations in that area. The allocation of 78 buses at the time of opening in 1977 made Cannock the largest garage on the system.

The loss of the Birmingham operations was reflected when, in March 1974, the official title was changed to Midland Red Omnibus Company Limited. A rather surprising reorganisation in December 1978 converted the last surviving garage in the Birmingham area, Digbeth, into a coach unit. This garage doubled as the Birmingham Coach Station and the exercise marked the beginning of the division of the company into compartments. All bus duties were transferred to garages further afield whilst, apart from a few vehicles at Cannock and Leicester, all coaches were concentrated at Digbeth. The garage also received the services, tours and contracts of the Midland garages of National Travel (West). The centralisation of coach work no doubt had some advantages but it did mean that Digbeth busmen found themselves as coach drivers, a different job entirely requiring a different attitude, whilst senior men at other garages lost the premier coaching work.

A significant development by the company was the Market Analysis Project, originally known as the Viable Network Project. The principle of MAP was that each garage should be able to support itself financially, with the network being slimmed until break-even was achieved. Routes were revised to meet the needs of as many passengers as possible. County councils, of course, were given the opportunity to add to this basic network by providing the necessary financial support. The principle was highly regarded by the counties because the company was able to say quite clearly which parts of the network required or did not require support.

The first MAP project to reach fruition was at Stratford-upon-Avon, in May 1977 and the new service network was marketed under the appropriate name of 'Avonbus'. MAP eventually spread throughout the NBC empire, into Scotland and was even promoted abroad, but it started life with Midland Red.

By 1981 the whole of the Midland Red system had received the attention of the MAP men and had been divided into handy compartments, each with an individual marketing name. The only exception was Leicester where services in the city were shared with the City Transport. In the writer's opinion, by being largely based on on-bus surveys, MAP had a serious deficiency. It met the needs of most existing passengers with the minimum number of vehicles and drivers, but had to dispense with those passengers that did not fit in. It paid minimal attention to seeking out new clientele which household based surveys would have discovered. MAP was thus a recipe for contraction, holding out little hope of compensatory expansion.

Midland Red had become like a sick man who had undergone a serious operation in 1973 and was now suffering from an appalling wasting disease. The fleet size had slumped to around 900 vehicles, half the total of 20 years previous. NBC had a number of subsidiaries in a similar condition, each with headquarters and works facilities that were under-utilised following the contractions. Midland Red became the company with a hole in the middle after the sale to West Midlands PTE. The remaining operations were so arranged that division would not be too difficult an exercise. Thus it was not a complete surprise when the announcement came in February 1981 that the company was to be divided up and the portions, whilst retaining the Midland Red name, placed under the care of adjacent NBC companies. The staff of Midland House and Carlyle Works were given notice of redundancy to take effect after 5 September 1981 when Midland Red, as we knew it, would come to an end. The reader is left to imagine the thoughts of those who, in many cases, had dedicated years to keeping their company afloat and were now faced with the prospect of joining the unemployment line at the height of the worst recession since the war.

Right: Stratford Blue had five of its outmoded 1950 Leyland Tiger PS2 saloons rebodied as double-deckers. Four received attractive Northern Counties bodies and survived to run for Midland Red. This mid-1960s Pool Meadow scene emphasises the close links between the two companies as 34 prepares to make a Coventry-Leamington journey on Midland Red's 517 service. LD8 No 4065 is to the rear. *Michael Dryhurst*

Below: Willowbrook bodies were chosen for most Stratford Blue Leyland Titans from 1956. 1960 PD3/4 No 30 and 1956 PD2/12 No 20 stand at the garage entrance on the first day of Midland Red operation, 1 January 1971. Midland Red added 2000 to the fleet numbers. *MRK*

Right: The oldest Stratford Blue buses to receive Midland Red livery were some of these Willowbrook-bodied Leyland Tiger Cubs, dating from 1959. No 2041 leaves the yard at the side of Stratford garage in February 1971. *B. L. Thompson*

Below: 1963 Northern Counties-bodied Leyland PD3/4 No 2025 awaits its next duty in the Red Lion yard which serves as Stratford's bus station. Midland Red sold the entire ex-Stratford Blue PD3 fleet, some 15 vehicles, in 1971/2 to Isle of Man Road Services, where they were re-registered. *Maurice Collignon*

Below right: Stratford garage, in both Blue and Red days, had an evening journey on the 154 Birmingham to Solihull service which subsequently passed to WMPTE. 1963 Willowbrook-bodied PD3A/1 No 2005 is seen in Shirley in July 1971. *MRK*

Right: Stratford vehicles were more usually seen in Birmingham on the 150 service, now replaced by limited stop facilities. 1965 Weymann-bodied Leyland PSU3 Leopard No 2054 tops Camp Hill, Birmingham, in June 1975. *MRK*

Below right: The Stratford Blue vehicle to give longest passenger service to Midland Red was this 1970 Alexander-bodied Leyland Leopard PSU3 coach. It ended up on service bus duties at Ludlow garage, surviving long enough to pass to Midland Red (North). No 2036 loads at Shrewsbury bus station in April 1982. *MRK*

Below: The company considered that the lightweight Ford R192 was man enough to replace ageing S14s and S15s on rural services. In any case, these vehicles were only intended to have a seven-year life before sale although, in the event, it was found necessary to overhaul some of them for extended service. No 6338, one of the initial batch of Plaxton-bodied 45-seat Fords received in 1970-1, shows off the cream waistband with which it was delivered as it loads in High Town, Bridgnorth, on town service B91 in August 1974. *MRK*

Left: 1971 saw the delivery of a large batch of 49-seat Willowbrook-bodied Leopards to dual-purpose specification. No 6414 was suffering from this all-over advertisement livery when seen at Stourbridge Town Station in December 1977. The bus had come from Worcester. Despite the cessation of manufacture of BMMO vehicles, the type classification system continued although the use of an initial letter for 'outside' makes was dropped. Succeeding batches of similar vehicles received different designations, and the introduction of new letters for Fords, Nationals, midibuses and dual-purpose buses confused matters, so the writer does not propose to refer to them for post-1970 stock. *MRK*

Below left: The last Leopards to a purely service bus specification were 13 with Marshall 53-seat bodies, received in 1972. No 6472, leaving Victoria bus station, Nottingham, in August of that year, was also the penultimate bus in the fleet numbering series adopted on vehicles from March 1944. The next batch of buses began a new series at 101. *G. H. F. Atkins*

Below: Four modified LC7 coaches, re-designated CM7A, succeeded the CM6s on the Birmingham-Worcester motorway services by early 1972. No 5785 shows the rather untidy arrangement of the power door as it draws away from Birmingham Bus Station in April 1972. The quartet passed to City of Oxford Motor Services in 1973. *Maurice Collignon*

EXPRESS SERVICE
BIRMINGHAM
THE IMPERIAL
BIRMINGHAM
LONDON
MOTORWAY
EXPRESS
5648
Midland Red
5648
Midland Red
BHA 648C

BIRMINGHAM
Midland Red
CHA 83C

We'll deliver everywhere
MIDLAND RED
CHA 418K
MIDLAND RED

Left: A start was made in 1972 on facelifting the CM6 family. No 5648 shows off its bus style destination indicators and deep polished moulding as it leaves Victoria Coach Station, London, in July 1972.
Maurice Collignon

Below left: Coaches began to receive National white livery in June 1972, initially with standard Midland Red lettering. LC7 No 5783 enters Digbeth Coach Station, Birmingham, in August of that year.
Maurice Collignon

Bottom left: Buses began to receive the now familiar NBC liveries later in 1972. An early repaint was this Leopard, No 6418, with red and white areas of the dual-purpose livery intriguingly transposed.
Maurice Collignon

Right: The narrow white relief band applied to buses was a welcome improvement even if the shade of red was a disappointment. Daimler Fleetline No 6035 passes through picturesque Henley-in-Arden during May 1976. *MRK*

Below: The single-deck application of the NBC livery is exemplified by No 5722, one of three dual-purpose prototypes produced in 1965. Originally classified S21A, they were later designated S22 but, by 1977 when this picture was taken in Colmore Row, Birmingham, they were humble S17s. *MRK*

Right: The Leyland National was produced in Cumberland by a new company, jointly owned by Leyland and NBC. In view of the latter's involvement, subsidiary companies were required after 1972 to take Nationals for their service bus needs. Early examples were not particularly reliable and gained the nickname 'Cumberland Dustbins'! However the manufacturers and operators persevered with the model which gradually improved. Several hundred entered Midland Red service including No 571, seen negotiating a narrow arch on a two-way road in Atherstone during April 1980. *S. Knight*

Below: Further batches of Fords were received, in NBC livery, for rural services until 1974. It then appeared that some Bristol LH models, the standard NBC lightweight bus, would be taken into stock in 1975. However the order was diverted, as was one for a batch of Leyland Atlantean double-deckers expected around the same time. An earlier order for no less than 118 Atlanteans for delivery in late 1971 and 1972, had also been diverted away from the Company. Ford No 163, at Pool Meadow, Coventry, in July 1978 stands alongside Leopard No 6429 on the long X91 Leicester to Hereford service, now dismembered. The Leopard had been downgraded from dual-purpose to service bus livery by this time. *MRK*

Left: No 353 is typical of the 100 Marshall-bodied PSU3 Leopards wearing dual-purpose livery received in 1973 and 1974. Attractive Tewkesbury is the location. *MRK*

Below left: The 413 buses sold to West Midlands PTE in December 1973 received new fleetnames immediately and, apart from those withdrawn fairly soon after the takeover, were repainted into blue and cream as soon as practicable. Red S17 No 5547 keeps it doors closed whilst awaiting departure time one chilly day at Dudley in February 1974. The next high point east of Dudley is apparently the Urals in Russia, which may explain the icy nature of the town in winter! The local service number D10 recalls a high spot of BMMO technology. *MRK*

Below: Buses repainted into WMPTE livery looked rather fine although the blue line applied at cantrail level to standard PTE double-deckers and only a few ex-BMMO vehicles would have helped to break up the area of cream on No 6215. It was one of many D13s converted to single entrance by the PTE and is seen in Priory Queensway, Birmingham, during July 1977 whilst working from the Sutton garage acquired from Midland Red. *MRK*

Above: The 1973 takeover of Green Bus of Rugeley brought a number of modern Seddons into the fleet. Seddon Pennine IV No 2154 was repainted into Midland Red colours but, like its sisters, was soon withdrawn and sold. It awaits a purchaser in May 1974 at Padmore Street garage, Worcester.
M. W. Greenwood

Above right: A number of Bedford coaches was acquired with the fleet of Cooper, Oakengates, in 1973 but only a couple ran for any length of time. The duo were Bedford YRQ models with Duple coach bodies which were converted for bus use and transferred to the ex-Harper garage at Heath Hayes. No 2147 was new in 1972 and is seen at Heath Hayes in January 1977. *MRK*

Right: Hoggins of Wrockwardine Wood was acquired in 1974. The fleet included this Plaxton-bodied Ford R192 which fitted in well with Midland Red's own buses of that make. XUX 417K, seen working for its original owner, became No 2181 in the Midland Red fleet.
Alan D. Broughall

Above: Withdrawn by Harper Brothers of Heath Hayes shortly before the 1974 takeover were these two 1951 Leyland Royal Tigers rebodied by the operator in 1960 using Metal Sections frames. BMMO also obtained its frames from the same firm and the resemblance of the sides to the S14 is remarkable, although the fronts are rather different. *Roy Marshall*

Below: Harper Brothers fares were extremely good value and the evening peak journey on the Birmingham-Cannock service required a duplicate which ran as far as Heath Hayes. Two ex-Harper Leyland Titans with Northern Counties bodies load in Carrs Lane, Birmingham, in July 1975. 1968 PD3A/1 No 2224 is the duplicate, scheduled to depart ahead of the Cannock bus, in this case the legendary 1962 PD2/28 No 2225, reputed to be the fastest double-decker in the area. No 2225 retains its Harper destination display. *MRK*

Above: Two 1970 Daimler Fleetlines with interesting and quite separate backgrounds, linked by history. Midland Red No 2230, with Northern Counties body, started life with Harper Brothers whilst Park Royal-bodied WMPTE No 3989 was part of an order placed by Wolverhampton Corporation before the takeover of its bus fleet. Both are on former Wolverhampton Corporation routes, the No 878 being one of a small number of country services to the north-west of Wolverhampton which passed to Midland Red when the PTE acquired the Company's Birmingham and Black Country operations. The opening by Midland Red of its Cannock garage in 1977, taking over the former Harper operations from Heath Hayes and the ex-Wolverhampton services from Cradley Heath, completed a chain of events which brought ex-Harper Fleetlines onto a service which was once Wolverhampton 52. Fordhouses terminus, on the West Midlands county boundary, in January 1978. *MRK*

Above right: Harper's newest double-deckers were two Leyland-engined Fleetlines with ECW bodies, dating from 1973. Two more ECW-bodied Fleetlines, ordered by Harper but with Gardner engines, went directly into the Midland Red fleet in 1976 as 439-40. The last mentioned, sporting National Holidays advertisements, awaits its next duty at Wolverhampton Bus Station in May 1982. *MRK*

Right: This Bedford SB5, built for Harper in 1972 with a distinctly conservative Willowbrook bus body, was nicknamed the 'Breadvan'. It is seen in November 1976 on the yard opposite the now closed garage at Heath Hayes, once a mecca for bus enthusiasts. *MRK*

Above: Harper Brothers bought Leyland Leopards for more arduous duties and these served Midland Red for rather longer than the Bedfords. 1972 Duple-bodied Leyland PSU3B/4R No 2252 loads at London Victoria for Coventry — the National Express lettering was adopted during the battle with independent operators after the deregulation brought about by the 1980 Transport Act. *Michael Dryhurst*

Left: The Bedford SB5 was a typical independent coachman's vehicle — cheap and rather noisy, but straightforward and reliable. This 1971 example with Duple body started out as Harper's No 58. The engine is at the front and it is ironic that truck derived machines like this should find their way into the fleet that pioneered underfloor-engined coaches a quarter of a century earlier. *M. Fowler*

Below left: The giant of both the Harper and Midland Red fleets was this 12m (39ft) Leyland Leopard PSU5/4R with Plaxton 55-seat body, built in 1973. No 2267 stands at Heath Hayes in November 1976. *MRK*

Above: Leyland PSU3 Leopards with Plaxton Supreme bodies were taken from 1976 in coach form and to bus grant specification for longer stage services. The potentially smart appearance of 1976-built No 458 has been reduced by missing wheel and grille trim. It is seen at The Crescent, Tewkesbury, near the Abbey, in June 1979. *MRK*

Right: Charge of the light brigade! A new service over restricted roads in Redditch and a requirement for small buses elsewhere led to the purchase of five 1974 Ford Transits with Dormobile 16-seat bodies from London Country in 1977. The first three filled a gap in the fleet numbers, Nos 441-3, vacant through the diversion of three Leopard coaches to South Wales Transport before delivery to Midland Red. When the other pair of Fords was acquired later in the year, the quintet were numbered together as Nos 2121-5. XPE 123N was still No 443 when seen at work in Redditch during July 1977, and subsequently became No 2123. *Mark Alexander*

Above: More substantial small buses were formed by the conversion to 'midibuses' of some full size Fords that were due for withdrawal, an enterprise recalling the days of vehicle building at Carlyle Road. Some Fords were similarly converted for other NBC subsidiaries. No 6391 was the first to be shortened; the 27-seater is seen amongst new town architecture at Redditch Transport Interchange in July 1978. *S. Knight*

Right: An October 1978 view of National Travel West Bedford YMT/Plaxton YUE 592S working the National Exhibition Centre shuttle service. Two months later the shuttle contract, along with other NT West operations in the area, passed to Midland Red. This Bedford was then loaned to Midland Red as its No 2592 until the end of the 1979 summer season — some similar Bedfords were actually added to stock. *MRK*

Below right: The lack of new double-deckers to replace older vehicles being withdrawn was causing increasing embarrassment in some areas. The receipt of some geriatric PMT Leyland Atlanteans and Daimler Fleetlines gave some hope but, in the event, only one briefly entered Midland Red service. No 2910, a 1962 Weymann-bodied Atlantean, proceeds along Burley Way, Leicester, in April 1979. *M. W. Greenwood*

Above: The 50th and 60th anniversaries of the company's formation were celebrated by splendid brochures. By 1979, however, Midland Red was in desperate trouble and there was little to write about to give optimism for the next 75 years. Fortunately the anniversary did not go unmarked as Fleetline No 6007 was turned out in a special livery to recall the earliest days of the company. It is seen loading at Pool Meadow, Coventry, in April 1980 — note the BET 'magnet' monogram on the side and front. *MRK*

Above right: The Plaxton Supreme had evolved into this handsome style by the time the 1979 Leopards were received. No 778 is seen with the later fleetname at Gloucester Green, Oxford, in March 1982. *MRK*

Right: Eighteen Leopards received in 1980 had dual-purpose Willowbrook bodies. By April 1982, 797 was finding employment on an Expressway service of Midland Red (East). *MRK*

Above: Numerically the last new vehicles to enter service with the old Midland Red were 25 National 2 buses, received in 1980. These took fleet numbers up to 831, and were part of a larger order truncated because of the Company's financial position and the shrinking requirement for vehicles. No 812 of Midland Red (North) received this automatic destination display early in 1982. Passengers at Shrewsbury Bus Station in April of that year peer at the display which did not show up well in the spring sunshine. *MRK*

Below: A surprise in May 1981 was the repainting of this elderly Leopard into National Express livery for use on contracts to assist the hard-pressed coach fleet. No 6398 is shown at Digbeth in August 1981, shortly before the vehicle was stolen and, unfortunately, damaged beyond economic repair. *MRK*

Divided We Stand

The company was split up as planned on 6 September 1981. Five new companies were formed with back-up facilities from adjacent NBC subsidiaries:

Company	*Base*	*Assisted by*
Midland Red (Express) Ltd	Digbeth	Bristol
Midland Red (East) Ltd	Leicester	Trent
Midland Red (North) Ltd	Cannock	Potteries
Midland Red (South) Ltd	Rugby	United Counties
Midland Red (West) Ltd	Worcester	Bristol

Many Midland House employees managed to find positions with the new companies but by no means all. The fine building remained with the NBC, however, who moved in some of their own staff from elsewhere. Carlyle Road 'Central' Works survived after a fight, but its future remains under review. 'Carlyle Works' is now a trading name of the old MROC company and must break even to survive. Its spare capacity is utilised by taking in 'outside' jobs, notably private coach and road freight vehicle overhauls and repairs, for which it has to compete commercially and has rapidly built up a good reputation.

A regrettable aspect of the last few months of the old company had been the incursions into traditional Midland Red territory by neighbouring NBC operators, not to mention the expected pressure from the independent sector. United Counties provided the biggest surprise by introducing a Northampton-Birmingham service. Fortunately, most of the new companies are blessed with a fresh vigour, benefiting from decentralised managements that can be more responsive to outside competition. It has required, however, a major mental readjustment to realise that the new companies are not related, except as NBC subsidiaries, and that they can be in competition with each other. The misconception that they are merely divisions of the old Midland Red, indulging in a cosmetic exercise, has had to be quickly dispelled. The need for this has led to two of the companies breaking away from the NBC directives on livery, which previously had been rigidly enforced throughout England and Wales.

There was immediately some revival of interest in double-deckers after the split, the first evidence being four ex-Trent Daimler Fleetlines which joined the North and West fleets in September 1981.

Much of the early news, however, was provided by Midland Red (East). A number of coaches had continued to be based at Leicester on work that had little connection with the Digbeth operations. Thus eight coaches were transferred from Express to East jurisdiction with effect from 1 January 1982. East's tiny coach fleet was strengthened by two secondhand Leyland Leopards from Cumberland in the spring of 1982. These were not the first secondhand vehicles for East, however, as six ex-London Transport Daimler Fleetlines had entered service in February. The most intriguing feature of these Fleetlines was their maroon livery, significantly darker than poppy or even BMMO red. This shade then became standard for East's buses as they were repainted and many welcomed the change although, without a relief colour, it threatened to look dull once the newness wore off. The Fleetlines replaced National single-deckers which passed to Midland Red (North). More batches of London Fleetlines subsequently followed and continued East's policy of substituting doubles for single-deckers. Only one local identity name, Lancer, was included in East's area and, in February 1982, its early demise was announced.

This was in sharp contrast to Midland Red (North) where from the summer of 1982, the old company fleetname began to be submerged completely in favour of the now well-established local identity titles — Chaserider, Hotspur, Mercian and Tellus. The bus grant coaches, upon repaint, became white whilst the older bus-styled dual-purpose Leopards, like ordinary service buses, became basically poppy red all over. However both buses and coaches received a contrasting stripe which enclosed the fleet name, the colours matching those used for the post-MAP advertising which had differed in each of the four cases. The combinations produced are surprisingly smart and the overall effect highly original. North also gained the favour of enthusiasts by its operation of a 'preserved' BMMO D9 on summer Sundays. Express ceased its presence at Cannock in 1982 and North acquired coaches in replacement.

In April 1982, the fleetname Midland Red West first appeared on its vehicles and shortly afterwards South followed suit. Local identity names generally have been retained in tandem with the modified fleetnames.

Express received in the summer of 1982 a dozen Leyland Leopards which had been delayed for some time by the coachbuilder, Willowbrook. These are similar to the 1980 batch but, being Express coaches, are in all-over white livery. Further modernisation has been achieved by the rebodying by ECW of four older Leyland Leopards which gained new registration numbers. The Express fleet was renumbered in January 1983 to avoid duplication with National Travel (West) coaches.

The standard NBC diet of National single-deckers, Tiger coaches and Olympian double-deckers may be expected for any future new vehicles the companies are able to afford. Greater variety may be on the horizon, however, as the 1982 Monopolies and Mergers Commission report on the bus industry recommended that the NBC should free itself from its links with the Leyland empire, a financial connection responsible for the NBC dependency on Leyland products. This has now been done and one looks forward to future surprises because, in the days when BMMO manufactured its own buses, did not the trade press say 'There's always something new from Midland Red!' The use of borrowed MAN articulated buses by West at Redditch in 1983 must be a step in this direction!

The creation of the five companies seemed an interim arrangement prior to total absorption by the old-established undertakings providing back-up facilities. This possibility is receding, perhaps, as the new companies impose their own identities. Some may yet disappear but, as policies vary so much between them, there seems little reason to assume that if one goes then the others will be at risk. Those responsible for the visual impact made by some companies through the imaginative appearance of their vehicles and publicity deserve particular admiration.

Following the evident success of the Midland Red partition, the NBC has split up more of its subsidiaries. Suddenly big is no longer beautiful. Division certainly concentrated the mind on survival and freed the local managements from some of the inertia suffered by large companies. There must remain, however, doubts about the division of the old company. For example one of the main 'economies', the closing of Carlyle Works, seems to have been avoided, thankfully for those who have dedicated their working lives to the establishment. In Birmingham, the split caused a muddle of company images and disintegrated presentations. Thus, in March 1983, the four bus companies launched 'Midland Express', one name and livery (white with yellow and red relief) for the network of limited stop services based on Birmingham. Some of the companies purchased secondhand coaches around this time to minimise the use of bus-styled dual-purpose Leyland Leopards on Midland Express services.

Following the fortunes of five companies should be more interesting than just one but, whatever the future may bring, good wishes must surround the men and women struggling to survive in an industry where, these days, the rewards are rarely great.

Below: This solitary Leyland Tiger with Plaxton 51-seat body was received by the old organisation but entered service with Midland Red (Express) as No 832 in September 1981. The Tiger was tracked down to Cardiff Bus Station in April 1982. ***MRK***

Left: Of the four secondhand ex-Trent Daimler Fleetlines with Alexander bodies received by the new companies in September 1981, three initially went to Midland Red (West) for use at Hereford. The fleet number of 2541, passing through St Peter's Square in April 1982, is a nostalgic reminder of the D1 prototype. The fourth went into service with Midland Red (North) initially at Ludlow. Both towns had become entirely single-deck under the old management. *MRK*

Below left: The era of the second-hand bus. An ex-Northern General Transport Leyland National, numbered 100, with Midland Red (South) loads at St Margaret's, Leicester, in March 1983 alongside one of the many Daimler Fleetlines acquired by Midland Red (East) from London Transport. The overhaul work on nearly all the Fleetlines was carried out by Carlyle Works and included new destination layouts and removal of the centre doors. *MRK*

Bottom left: The first new Midland Red double-deckers for 12 years were 10 ECW-bodied Leyland Olympians for Midland Red (North) which came in summer 1983. No 1908, in Chaserider livery, is seen entering Colmore Row in July 1983. *MRK*

Below: One of four older Leyland Leopards fitted with new ECW bodies in 1983 for Midland Red (Express). No 552, undergoing a test run in the Bull Ring in May 1983, was once better known as 6255 (WHA 255H). *MRK*

Anywhere in the Midlands

A useful member of the Midland Red range of travel opportunities for many years was the 'Day Anywhere' card. Whilst the 'Day Anywhere' description was something of an exaggeration, use of the cards being restricted to Midland Red bus services, the holder did have access to the 12,000sq miles of the company's territory, much of which is of considerable scenic interest.

The use of special cards ceased when fare increases became a regular event, nowadays those wishing to explore without restriction the Midland Red area receive a selection of Setright tickets. It is still a good way for the youthful bus enthusiast to discover more about a fascinating bus operation and, at the same time, hopefully develop an appreciation of the region's towns and countryside. For those with an ear for such things, the Midlands embraces a wide range of accents, attractive or otherwise. The Birmingham man, for example, would have difficulty in understanding his counterpart just down the road in the Black Country. Both would have to listen carefully to the country chirrup of the Cotswolds and even the latter pales away against the ripe, rural tones of Herefordshire . . . One bus company covering all these accents and more!

It was reckoned that the holder of a 'Day Anywhere' card could clock up 300 miles by using some forward planning. The reader is now invited to take a trip right round the Midland Red area through the medium of photographs — a tour which would have been impossible on a single 'Day Anywhere' card. Particular attention is paid to the town services, with their special prefix letters. These prefixes were adopted from 1928, either as Midland Red opened up local services in a town, or by renumbering from the main series.

The territory is now split up between four companies, not counting the Express operations. At the end of this photographic tour, the reader may be left with the impression that North has the architecture, West the scenery, South the tourists, and East the passengers. A gross generalisation, of course, but one which may have more than a grain of truth in it.

Below: Birmingham remains the hub of Midland Red coach operations even if the bus presence has diminished. Great Charles Street was an important starting point for tours at one time — this view of the thoroughfare must date from around 1928. Not long after the opening of Digbeth garage in 1929, it began to be used for long distance departures, purely as a temporary measure. Separate premises were never acquired and Digbeth, somewhat improved, remains in use as Birmingham's Coach Station. *Midland Red*

Above left: Midland Red buses sold to West Midlands PTE sometimes found their way onto the services radiating from Birmingham centre inherited from the former City Transport undertaking. Just about the busiest is the 50 service and Leopard No 5212 is seen on a short working in June 1976. *MRK*

Below: The affluent area of Solihull, to the south-east of Birmingham, had its own local services although it was not until 1966 that the S prefix was first used here. S17 No 5732 loads in High Street, Solihull, during July 1975, after the WMPTE takeover. *MRK*

Above: To the north of Birmingham lies Sutton Coldfield, incorporated into the City in 1974. There was a more extensive network of local services here, the first use of the S prefix being September 1937. This Daimler Fleetline, seen in September 1965, looks ordinary enough but in fact No 5261 was fitted with a BMMO 10.5litre engine. *Maurice Collignon*

Below: Further north still is Tamworth which has been greatly expanded in recent years, strengthening its links with the West Midlands conurbation, although well outside that county. Tamworth is now served by the 'Mercian' network of Midland Red (North). National No 530 circumnavigates the Old Square, Birmingham, in April 1982 and advertised the 'Mercian Metrocard' which, once purchased, permits free travel in Tamworth and half price to elsewhere. *MRK*

Above: Midland Red operations in Birmingham itself also featured some prefix lettered services. These comprised the Dudley Road group of routes, jointly operated by the Company and Birmingham City Transport, an arrangement begun upon replacement of the Dudley Road tramcars in October 1939. The joint operation was more theoretical than real because each service in the group was generally run by only one of the undertakings. This scene at the then unloading stop in Birmingham, Margaret Street, shows D7 No 4546 on the B87 from Dudley, a completely BMMO preserve, whilst BCT Leyland PD2/Park Royal No 2199 is working the B82, almost entirely the Corporation's responsibility. The B prefix was dropped in June 1968, shortly after this photograph was taken, and the whole group now belongs to WMPTE. *MRK*

Below: BCT did not have complete possession of the B82, however, as shown by FEDD No 2372, ready for action on the service at Bearwood Bus Station in August 1955. *W. A. Camwell*

Above right: Colour cover of an interesting 48-page guide to residential districts throughout the Midlands. The FEDD and the evocative artwork date the booklet as the mid-thirties. The guide quite happily recommends the municipal transport of Birmingham — 'the city is faithful to its trams, and the fares have been got down to an almost unbelievably cheap level. For twopence or so you can go clanging your way home five miles out to the city boundary'.

Below left: The X number series was generally used for longer distance stage services, usually with stopping and/or minimum fare restrictions. However some odds and ends crept into the series, in particular some works and hospital services. There was also a number of holiday period only services to popular scenic destinations. One such service was the X82 and LD8 No 4002 is seen loading for Kinver via Stourbridge at Navigation Street, Birmingham, on a Bank Holiday Monday. *F. W. York*

Above left: Stourbridge also had S-prefixed local services, their first use in the town dating from January 1936. D5B No 3814 was working the S50 to High Park in August 1965 which involved, on the return journey, a tortuous right turn around an inadequate island from Park Road into Swan Street. The writer was once informed somewhat unkindly that, due to the age of its patrons, this service needed a fleet of ambulances rather than a bus. *Maurice Collignon*

Above: West Midlands PTE has disposed of all the prefix letters it inherited from Midland Red, either during service revisions or by straight renumbering into the PTE system. Stourbridge local services were extensively revised by the PTE in December 1976. D9 No 5422, working service 298 in September 1977, labours up the long gradient of Brook Holloway that, as often as not, would reduce a double-decker to first gear. This section of road was served by the S47 at the time of takeover. *MRK*

Left: The route board over the bonnet gives the true destination of FEDD No 2355, seen at Stourbridge Town Station whilst making a Kidderminster to Wolverhampton journey on service 885 in May 1959. *F. W. York*

Above: A typical Black Country scene as S9 No 3456, fully laden, tackles Quarry Bank in July 1963. These early postwar saloons would 'chuff' as higher revs were reached and the governor cut in, and no doubt No 3456 showed that delightful characteristic during this climb. A cyclist is able to take momentary advantage of the S9's slipstream.
Alan D. Broughall

Below right: D prefix letters were introduced to Dudley in October 1934. Petrol FEDD No 1565 works one of the Priory Estate locals, the D11, but the D stencil is missing. *R. A. Mills*

Below: Dudley provided the greatest visual change when the PTE took over, Midland Red having been clearly the majority presence in the town until December 1973. This interesting view taken in February 1974 shows Fleetline No 5277, fresh in its new PTE colours, loading for Wolverhampton. Behind is S22 No 5881 with S17 grille, still working for Midland Red on service X93, one of the X96 family of routes soon to be diverted via the motorway and removing the last vestige of regular company operation in the town. The 125 was routed via the New Wolverhampton Road, opened by the Prince of Wales in November 1927. It is recorded that, as the Prince cut the tapes at the various boundaries, Midland Red buses began running immediately to take the crowds home. *MRK*

Bottom: Interesting line-up at Stafford including AD2 No 3161 and FEDDs Nos 1808 and 1796, all with Metro-Cammell bodies — the S prefix was first used in the town in 1946. Stafford is now part of the 'Chaserider' network, which also embraces operations from Cannock garage.

IRONBRIDGE
via MADELEY
897
MIDLAND
NHA 664
W41
LHA 375

COPTHORNE
2324
MIDLAN
FHA
479

Above left: This new garage at Wellington, opened in September 1953, replaced earlier premises on the same site. At the entrance, S9 No 3375 prepares to work Wellington schools service W41 whilst S10 No 3664 leaves for Ironbridge. When Midland Red (North) assumed control, Wellington was handling the Telford-based 'Tellus' services and part of the 'Hotspur' network. *Midland Red*

Left: Shrewsbury, the county town of Shropshire, is a treasurehouse of half-timbered buildings situated within a loop of the River Severn. Rebuilt SON 2324 stands in the bus station whilst working local services. Rowley's House in the background dates from the early 16th century. *Robert F. Mack*

Above: D5B No 3783, with non-standard upper deck front vents, works town service S1 in March 1963. The prefix letter was introduced to Shrewsbury in June 1934. *C. J. Davis*

Below: 'Hotspur' National No 295 climbs up from Shrewsbury railway station in April 1982. To show how obscure local identity names can get, the title of the network, introduced in November 1979, recalls the Yorkist champion, Sir Henry Percy — otherwise known as Harry Hotspur — who was killed at the Battle of Shrewsbury in 1403. *MRK*

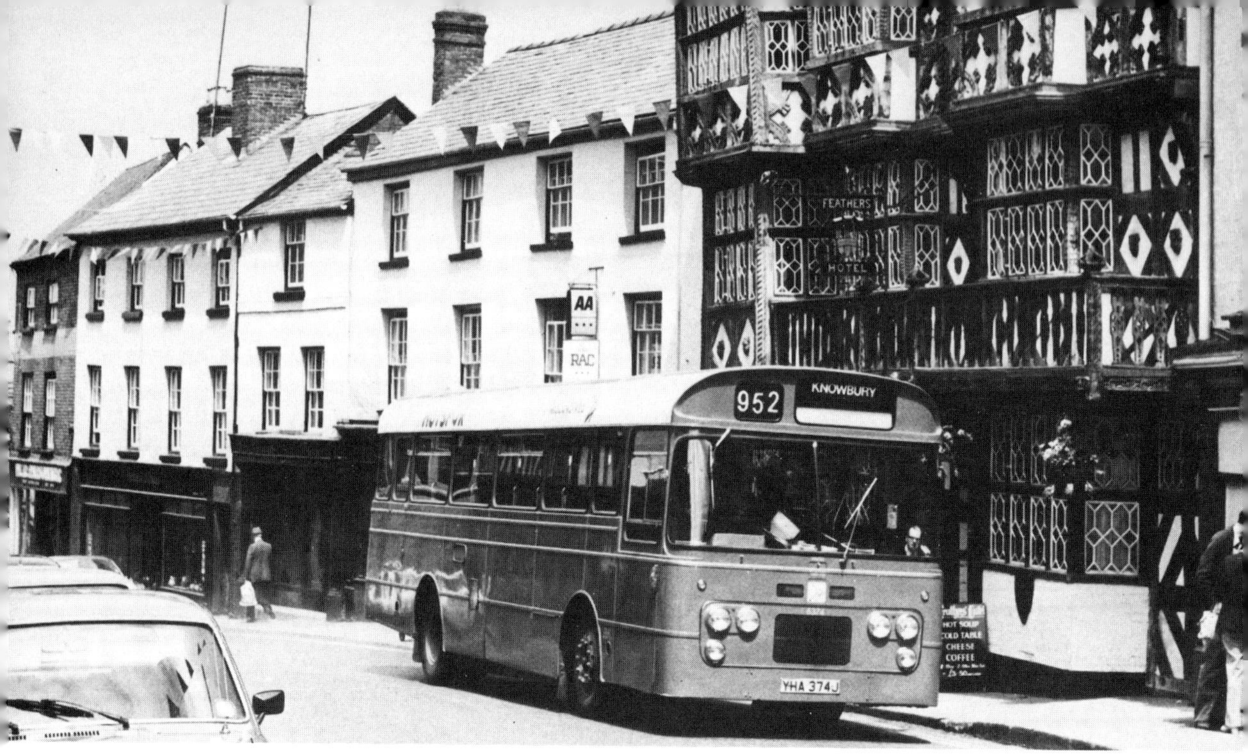

Above: Ludlow is also included in the 'Hotspur' network. The town was in festival mood as Ford R192 No 6374 passes the 17th century Feathers Hotel in June 1981. *MRK*

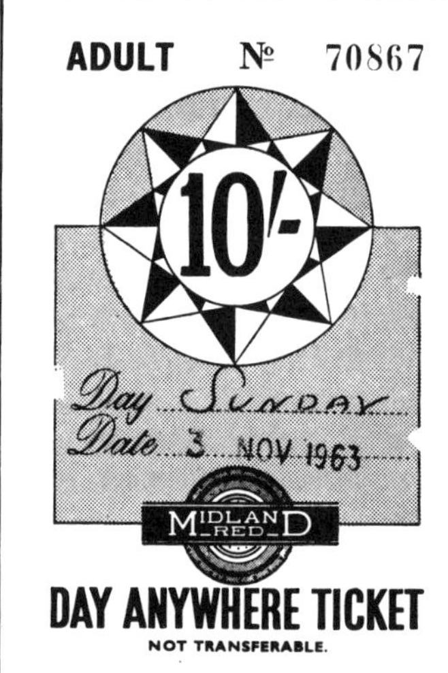

ADULT №70867

10/-

Day Sunday

Date 3 NOV 1963

MIDLAND RED

DAY ANYWHERE TICKET

NOT TRANSFERABLE.

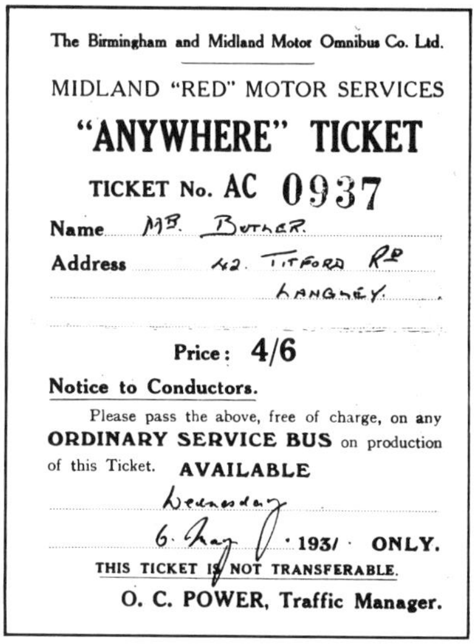

The Birmingham and Midland Motor Omnibus Co. Ltd.

MIDLAND "RED" MOTOR SERVICES

"ANYWHERE" TICKET

TICKET No. AC 0937

Name Mr. Butler

Address 42. Titford Rd

Langley.

Price: 4/6

Notice to Conductors.

Please pass the above, free of charge, on any ORDINARY SERVICE BUS on production of this Ticket. AVAILABLE

Wednesday

6 May 1931 ONLY.

THIS TICKET IS NOT TRANSFERABLE.

O. C. POWER, Traffic Manager.

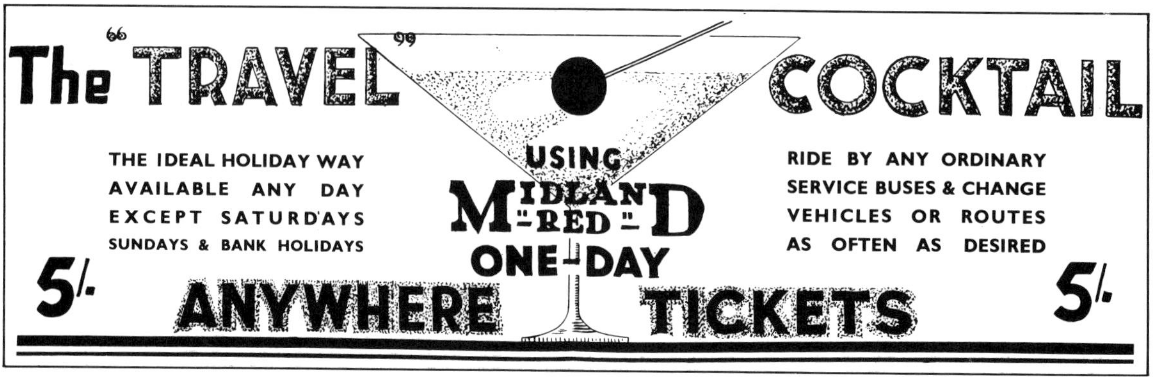

The "TRAVEL" COCKTAIL

THE IDEAL HOLIDAY WAY
AVAILABLE ANY DAY
EXCEPT SATURDAYS
SUNDAYS & BANK HOLIDAYS

USING
MIDLAND "RED"
ONE-DAY

RIDE BY ANY ORDINARY
SERVICE BUSES & CHANGE
VEHICLES OR ROUTES
AS OFTEN AS DESIRED

5/- ANYWHERE TICKETS 5/-

Above: The population of Bridgnorth is split between the Low Town, on the banks of the Severn, and the High Town. This country market town has a number of delights, including the tower of the castle keep which out-leans the Tower of Pisa. The rail enthusiast is kept occupied by the cliff railway linking the two parts of the town and, of course, by the Severn Valley Railway with its magnificent steam operated line to Bewdley. The SVR has yet to penetrate as far as Kidderminster but S17 No 5718, at Northgate in the High Town, was offering a direct facility in August 1974. *MRK*

Below: Prefix letters were introduced to Kidderminster in November 1931 and the town is now served by the 'Wendaway' network of Midland Red (West). This April 1967 view shows S15 No 5065 and S14 No 4715 working local services from the Post Office.
Maurice Collignon

Above: S13 No 3878 was the only one with a Willowbrook body and was a familiar sight at Hereford for many years. It is seen in the bus station in June 1960. *Alan D. Broughall*

Below: Midland Red services around Hereford have been severely pruned in recent years. The handful of remaining country services have left the bus station, now largely the preserve of Yeomans Motors, to join some of the local services terminating in St Peter's Square. As if the Company did not have enough to contend with, Hereford became a 'trial area' devoid of normal licensing procedures. This resulted in Whitehead (Flashes Coaches) of Newent competing with the Company over certain local services which hold out the only hope of any financial return in the cathedral city. Here, in April 1982, Whitehead's ex-Leicester Bristol RELL/ECW TRY 123H is abstracting custom from MR (West) 'Wandaward' service H17 to Newton Farm. Both drivers are dealing with passenger enquiries — any confusion is perhaps understandable. *MRK*

Right: The original March 1920 timetable issued in Hereford.

MIDLAND 'RED' MOTOR OMNIBUSES

ARE NOW RUNNING TO AND FROM

HEREFORD AT THE FOLLOWING TIMES:

Hereford, Credenhill & Weobley Route.

WEEKDAYS. SUNDAYS.
HEREFORD (High Town) Depart 9-30 a.m. 3-5 p.m. 2-0 p.m. 6-0 p.m.
WEOBLEY (Post Office) ,, 11-0 a.m. 4-30 p.m. 3-20 p.m. 7-20 p.m.
Extra Journey to CREDENHILL on Saturdays only 8-0 p.m.

Hereford, Clehonger & Madley Route.

WEEKDAYS. SUNDAYS.
HEREFORD, Depart 12-45 p.m. 6 p.m. 4-40 p.m. 9-0 p.m.
MADLEY, ,, 1-35 p.m. 6-45 p.m. 5-20 p.m. 9-40 p.m.

Hereford, Much Birch & Ross Route.

Mondays, Wednesdays, Thursdays & Saturdays. SUNDAYS.
HEREFORD, Depart 9-0 a.m. 2-10 p.m. 3-15 p.m. 7-45 p.m.
ROSS (George Hotel) Depart 10-20 a.m. 4-10 p.m. 4-45 p.m. 9-10 p.m.

Hereford, Mordiford & Fownhope Route.

WEEKDAYS. SUNDAYS.
HEREFORD, Depart 8-30 a.m. (W) 12-30 p.m. 5-35 p.m. 1-45 p.m. 6-15 p.m.
FOWNHOPE, ,, 9-0 a.m. 1-15 p.m. 6-20 p.m. 2-30 p.m. 7-0 p.m.
"W" Wednesdays and Saturdays only.

Hereford, Bodenham & Leominster Route.

Tuesdays and Fridays only.
HEREFORD, Depart 9 a.m. 2 p.m. LEOMINSTER (Corn Square), Depart 10-20 a.m. 3-30 p.m.

Hereford, Lugwardine & Ledbury Route.

WEEKDAYS ONLY.

HEREFORD, Depart	W 8-35 a.m.	2-20 p.m.	W 3-0 p.m.	7-30 p.m.
LUGWARDINE, Arrive		2-35 p.m.		7-45 p.m.
LEDBURY, Depart	W 10-0 a.m.		W 4-30 p.m.	
LUGWARDINE, Depart		2-40 p.m.		8-0 p.m.
HEREFORD, Arrive	11-10 a.m.	2-55 p.m.	5-40 p.m.	8-15 p.m.

"W" Wednesdays and Saturdays only.

Hereford & Widemarsh Common (Saturdays Only).

HIGH TOWN, Depart 7-5 p.m. 7-35 p.m. 8-5 p.m. 8-35 p.m. 9-5 p.m.
WIDEMARSH COMMON, Depart 7-20 ,, 7-50 ,, 8-20 ,, 8-50 ,, 9-20 ,,

The Company will make every effort to maintain these Services, but reserve the right to alter, suspend, or withdraw any vehicle or service without notice, and will accept no liability for loss, damage, injury, or delay, sustained by any passenger by reason of unpunctuality or failure to maintain Service.

O. C. Power, Traffic Manager.

Motor Omnibus Garages: 547, Bearwood Road, Smethwick (Tel. No. 2577 Midland).
Black Lion Hotel, Hereford (Tel. No.).

Birmingham & Midland Motor Omnibus Co., Ltd.

March, 1920, and until further notice.

4031

The first time-table issued at Hereford—March 1920.

Above: The only surviving service between Hereford and Worcester is the 420 via the attractive market town of Bromyard. This early postwar view shows two S10s in the town, the leading vehicle being No 3624.
Michael Rooum

Below: Another route between Hereford and Worcester was via Ledbury but this is no longer possible by Midland Red whose operations from the town have dwindled to an occasional link with Malvern. In the happier but, by the look of it, hardly more profitable days of March 1964, Hereford-based S8 No 3265 is about to make a journey on the Ledbury-Ross 472 service. Across the road is S14 No 4337, supplied by Malvern garage, working a Tuesday market day 417 journey to Cradley. The background gives some hint of this market town's attractiveness. The poet John Masefield was born here and his description of the town — 'pleasant to the sight, fair and half-timbered houses black and white' — is still valid today. *C. J. Davis*

Above left: S14 No 4255, still crew operated in July 1968, waits at Great Malvern Post Office, nestling below the Malvern Hills. A short climb from here permits an excellent view across the Severn and Avon to Bredon Hill whilst today's Leopards and Nationals remain clearly audible from below. A rather greater expenditure of energy will be rewarded by magnificent views westwards towards Wales. *Maurice Collignon*

Left: The once extensive network of Malvern local services (the M prefix was introduced in January 1935) supported a garage here until 1976. S15 No 5077 proceeds through Abbey Gateway, Great Malvern, in July 1968. This is now a pedestrian area.
Maurice Collignon

Below: The M services are now a memory and what is left of Malvern's local demand is met by the 'Severnlink' network based on Worcester, run by Midland Red (West). Early National No 124 loads in Church Street, Great Malvern, during April 1982.
MRK

Above: The principle of prefix letters was established in Worcester when Midland Red buses succeeded the tramcars on 1 June 1928. S17 No 5615 waits at Angel Place, in the centre of Worcester, in September 1966. *Maurice Collignon*

Below: The first use of a marketing name on the Midland Red system was at Redditch where services were extensively revised to cater for the large new housing developments in the area. This was the ideally titled 'Reddibus' network, introduced in March 1976, which was accompanied by different types of 'Redditickets'. Nationals, including No 485 seen in July 1977, received this special 'Reddibus' lettering on the sides. A pity most subsequent marketing names could not recapture the originality of 'Reddibus'. The use of the R prefix predated the new network by a wide margin, however, being first employed in 1934. *MRK*

Right: Evesham, at the centre of a fruit-growing region, had its own local services, the E prefix being introduced in February 1946. D9 No 4941, one of two with 'hopper' rather than sliding side ventilators, works the E3 in April 1970.
Alan D. Broughall

Below right: The MAP planners visited Evesham very early on, the 'Wayfarer' network being introduced in July 1977. All services in the new network were numbered in a series previously associated with Midland Red's Black Country operations, and so the E prefix departed. The withdrawal of 'rural' buses like the Fords, and the interworking of routes to achieve maximum economy of operation, has meant the appearance of high quality specification vehicles in unlikely places. Leyland Leopard/Plaxton No 666 provides luxurious accommodation on service 254 to Honeybourne in November 1981. The elegance of the town remains obvious despite the wintry gloom.
MRK

Bottom right: FEDD No 2128 offers a ride of exceptional beauty from Stratford-upon-Avon to Evesham via the mellow, honey-coloured Cotswold stone villages of Chipping Campden and Broadway. Alongside the FEDD a large notice advertises the various enterprises of both Stratford Blue and Midland Red — your enquiries solicited. Impressive signwriting such as this is now impossible to maintain in the era of the spraycan and disrespect for property in public places. *Robert F. Mack*

Above: Stratford Blue service 44 ran to Oxford, a joint operation with City of Oxford Motor Services. Midland Red (South), still jointly with the Oxford undertaking, nowadays provide the X50 Oxford-Stratford-Birmingham limited stop facility. Double-deckers remain a regular sight on the route — Fleetline No 6273 has just arrived at the Gloucester Green bus station, Oxford, in September 1979. In May 1977, Stratford had been the first area to receive the MAP treatment — the 'Avonbus' promotional name is clearly seen. *MRK*

Below: Stratford-upon-Avon, an old market town and, of course, the birthplace of William Shakespeare, offers many buildings of interest and, in the summer months, arguably more tourists per square mile than London. Until 1971 its local services and many country routes were provided by Stratford Blue. Midland Red buses were familiar in the town on other country routes, however, including S10 No 3614 on its way to Bromsgrove. *A. Hustwitt*

Right: The company's services in Banbury began in October 1919 with, as in so many other towns, the despatch of three vehicles, the minimum of manpower and a supply of handbills to post through letterboxes advising folk that Midland Red buses would be running from the next day — enraging the proprietors of horse-drawn carrier carts which plied regularly to and from the town, particularly on market days. The B prefix was first used in July 1933 and the present local identity name of 'Ridercross' delightfully recalls the famous Banbury Cross and the nursery rhyme associated with it. AD2 No 3101 pulls away from one of the town centre stances used before the opening of the bus station. *Alan B. Cross*

Below right: Royal Leamington Spa, with its fine Georgian architecture, and neighbouring Warwick, the county town with its 14th century castle, Tudor and still more Georgian buildings, were first served by L-prefixed local services when Midland Red took over from the Leamington & Warwick Transport Company on 1 October 1937. Now the wheel has almost gone full circle as the local identity name 'Leamington & Warwick' was adopted after MAP. Leamington was the home for most of its life of No 3877, the first production S13, one of only two with Carlyle-built bodies. It is seen at Warwick Square in October 1961. *Alan D. Broughall*

Bottom right: Coventry, an important city since the 14th century, is close enough to Stratford to be included on the tourist circuit. Forty acres of the attractive old city centre were levelled in a single air raid in November 1940. Whether the handful of surviving medieval buildings and the host of modern structures, including the much vaunted cathedral, warrant so much attention from the travel trade is open to question. For the Midland Red afficionado, the city is notable as a meeting place of several MAP networks, including that of Rugby, now the responsibility of Midland Red (South). National No 409, loading at Pool Meadow, Coventry, in September 1981, advertises the Rugby network — the layout of its red and white livery gives the false impression that this is a dual-purpose bus. *MRK*

Above: Coventry has long had a link to Tamworth via Nuneaton — see the FS on page 17. The X77 is a modern day facility, limited stop between Coventry and Nuneaton. Leopard/Willowbrook No 6394 leaves Pool Meadow in August 1981 with its Nuneaton-based 'Hunter' name clearly visible. Pool Meadow Bus Station was opened in October 1931. *MRK*

Left: Weymann-bodied Leopard No 5168 and S23 No 5939 wait for customers during August 1977 in Nuneaton's spacious bus station, opened in May 1956. The N prefix was first used in May 1932 — today's 'Hunter' network is under the wing of Midland Red (South). *MRK*

Below left: Both Hinckley's H prefix, first seen in March 1935, and its garage have become Midland Red history. New Leopard/Marshall No 6468 loads at Hinckley's Bus Station in September 1972. *Maurice Collignon*

Above: Leicester, particularly associated with the footwear and hosiery trades, is a county town, a cathedral city boasting a fine shopping centre and its own municipal bus fleet. Midland Red (East) also has a large number of services, local and otherwise, centred upon the city which, until recently, supported three company garages. The L prefix was introduced for local services in February 1932, but was subsequently abandoned as co-ordination with the corporation increased. The grim concrete shelters, recently the subject of facelifting attempts, of St Margarets Bus Station are a familiar background to views of Midland Red buses in Leicester. The Bus Station was opened, in an incomplete state, in July 1942. AD2 and D5 buses had the tops of their windscreens raised early in life but this was not possible on No 3483 because, curiously, it appears to have an extra heater intake. *G. H. F. Atkins*

Right: Another important Leicester terminus was The Newarke. There used to be plenty of D5s in the city; here in July 1963 No 3485 has just overtaken No 3854. *Alan D. Broughall*

Above left: To the north-west of Leicester lies Coalville, where C prefix local services first appeared on the last day of 1938. D7 No 4514 loads for Ibstock in October 1963. *Maurice Collignon*

Left: Some MAP schemes meant the end of prefix letters but the 'Lancer' network brought them back to Coalville, albeit with different numbers, after they had been abandoned previously. 'Lancer' was the only local identity name within the Midland Red (East) empire and has therefore been allowed to fade away. Shoppers board National No 494 in Coalville during August 1981. *MRK*

Service Extended

Right: HA 4838 found further employment, along with fellow QL HA 4890, as a trainee vehicle until 1952. This spot, then immediately opposite the Company's driving school at Bearwood, was the starting point for many a hopeful driver.

Below: The training fleet was modernised in 1952 with some newer vehicles, converted to dual-control. One machine was SON CHA 551, a member of the 1936 English Electric-bodied batch with side, rather than rear, emergency door. A full width cab has been fitted and the fuel tank moved further back but otherwise the body is largely as originally built. A white-knuckled potential driver pilots the machine along Hagley Road, Birmingham. It was withdrawn in 1962. *Alan D. Broughall*

Top: Two 1937 SLRs were converted to dual-control trainers in 1955 and, like the SON left, were replaced by C1s in the early 1960s. CHA 962 ran until 1963 and just missed the preservation era — a sad loss. The SLR is seen waiting at Bearwood to intimidate a new recruit. *Alan D. Broughall*

Above: The company has produced tree cutters from a wide variety of former bus types. SOS Q HA 3653 performed this valuable function from 1936 until 1947. A team is seen at work in Bristol Road, Bournbrook, Birmingham, in October 1939.

Top right: An attractive 1953 conversion of 1937 SON DHA 648 which served for 10 years in this form. Foliage requiring trimming would have been hard to find at the time of this snow-covered scene. *G. H. Stone*

Right: The tree cutting fleet was again modernised in 1963 with three S9s and one D5. The former No 3385 is seen at work between Great Malvern and Malvern Wells in June 1965. *C. J. Davis*

Above: The last D7s were withdrawn in 1972, apart from No 4114 which hung on until 1973. Eleven of the final survivors were converted to towing vehicles, the work being carried out to several styles at a number of company establishments. Why the management suddenly felt the need for all these towing lorries is open to speculation! This example belonged to Shrewsbury. *Maurice Collignon*

Below: The D7s have been succeeded by Leyland Leopards, particularly the short wheelbase 1966 LC9s with their pre-Elite styling and low seating capacity which would have depressed their sale value. They have made very attractive towing vehicles, however — here, on the outskirts of Brownhills in February 1982, the crew of Cannock's example attend to ex-Harper CRG6 No 2230 whilst CRL6 No 2234 assumes the work of the disabled vehicle. *MRK*

Carlyle Road Works

All major maintenance and repairs were initially handled at Bearwood garage but the expansion of the fleet and the moves into body and then chassis manufacture led the company to purchase a seven-acre site off Carlyle Road, Edgbaston, Birmingham.

The site was acquired in two stages from the Daimler Co Ltd, who had used it for the manufacture of aircraft. A substantial part, purchased in September 1920, enabled body overhaul, construction and repair work to be carried out at Carlyle Road. The remainder followed in November 1924, after which new chassis were assembled there. Chassis and engine overhauls, and all experimental work, remained the responsibility of Bearwood.

Little alteration was made to the collection of buildings at this time but the division of work between Carlyle Road and Bearwood was inconvenient. However, the war years saw the same breadth of foresight applied to the works facilities as to vehicle development, and plans were drawn up for an extensive reconstruction of Carlyle Road when the war ended. The desperate shortage of materials in the early postwar years slowed matters somewhat but BMMO was proudly able formally to open its Central Works, as Carlyle Road now became known, for the company's 50th anniversary in 1954. The many new features of the works were widely acclaimed in the technical press and throughout the bus industry. The company was now able to concentrate all major work on one site and resume the assembly of new bus bodies. Bodywork produced by the company has been described as 'Carlyle' throughout this book.

The threatened future of the works from 1981 has been detailed in earlier chapters. It is interesting to note, however, that the name 'Carlyle Works' was adopted when the company began to seek outside business in its battle to keep the works open.

Above: The paint spraying booth, introduced in 1954, could deal with a double-decker within 12min. A resprayed bus then passed to a drying chamber where it would be 'baked'. The finishing section then got to work, applying transfers, cleaning windows, fitting destination blinds etc. Here an army of ladies (including Mary, see bucket by front wheel) tackle a D5 in 1954 during the short period between the introduction of spray painting and the abandonment of yellow lining.
Midland Red

Below: A number of prewar vehicles plus an AD2 undergo attention over the chassis repair pits in 1954.
Midland Red

Red Sunset

Until recently, retired Midland Red vehicles rarely found further use with other operators. SOS and BMMO spares were not widely obtainable and, in any case, the buses had always run up an enormous mileage even if their lives were not particularly long. Notable exceptions were many of the SLR Leyland-engined coaches which found new homes abroad, whilst showmen took a shine to the slogging capabilities of the SOS and, with their customary ability to make do and mend, kept them on the road despite the spares difficulties. The occasional BMMO entered service with a new owner, D9s in particular turned up in some interesting places.

Second homes for stock of outside manufacture were more numerous. Many of the wartime buses, sold after barely a decade of service and with the worst aspects of austerity mellowed by rebuilding, interested a number of independents and operators of staff transport. Nowadays news of a further owner for a Midland Red vehicle rarely raises eyebrows as shorter lives with the company were intended for the coach fleet, which needs to be kept up-to-date, and for the Ford single-deckers.

Above: An elderly retired dual-control trainer was an unusual choice for a hospitality vehicle. The former No 3311 was still in use in this capacity, however, for Arnold, Brierley Hill, in August 1978 and, hardly surprisingly, it has since been saved for preservation. *MRK*

Below: A small number of early postwar single-deckers was bought by Hulley's, the Derbyshire independent based in Baslow. S9 No 3400 is seen in June 1964. Hulley subsequently bought a C5 and the ex-Sheffield Leopards. *Alan D. Broughall*

Above: D9s have cropped up in some surprising places, the best publicised being the examples converted to open top and operated on London sightseeing tours by Obsolete Fleet. The South Wales independent, Morris of Pencoed, also bought a few — the former Nos 4965 and 5017 being seen here in Morris's blue livery in January 1975. *MRK*

Left: A number of 1963 Daimler Fleetlines was acquired by fellow NBC subsidiaries City of Oxford and Potteries Motor Traction. Some of the Oxford examples were painted in this striking blue and white scheme for the city's Park & Ride service. Oxford No 920 (ex-Midland Red No 5276) proceeds along Cornmarket Street in September 1979. *MRK*

Left: Many of the Fords which were sold after seven years' service with Midland Red found buyers in the independent sector. No 173 did not stray far, being purchased by Stevensons of Uttoxeter and seen here at their Spath premises in March 1981. *MRK*

Below: On the face of it a strange machine to close a book on Midland Red but underneath that continental coachwork lurks a familiar chassis. Former LC7 class Leyland Leopards Nos 5809 and 5813 were acquired by Heyfordian, their bodies scrapped and the chassis overhauled and modernised. They were then fitted with new Van Hool coach bodies and re-registered TWL 542 and 541T respectively. A number of independents dealt with Leopards in this way, providing the clients with apparently new coaches at a reduced cost — and, of course, the idea eventually spread to Midland Red (Express) who rebodied four Leopards in 1983 with new ECW coachwork. *MRK*